Moments for moms II

Peace, Patience, and Balance

VISIONARY:

Juanita N. Woodson

CO-AUTHORS

Shacre Jones	Letricia A. Brown
Tanisha T. Graves	Ivy Gray
Crystal D. Harrison	Lisa Freeman
Katelyn Lewis	Ronjeanna Harris
Sydney E. Scott	Nikki Lawrence
Sabrina L. Clemons	Lessie Harrison
Tyresha Baine	Cyteese Alexander

Moments for Moms II: Peace, Patience, and Balance

VISIONARY: JUANITA N. WOODSON

FOREWARD: TANESHIA YERBY

CO-AUTHORS
CRYSTAL D. HARRISON
LISA FREEMAN
SABRINA L. CLEMONS
TANISHA T. GRAVES
SYDNEY E. SCOTT
KATELYN B. SAUNDERS
TYRESHA BAINE
LETRICIA A. BROWN
NIKKI LAWRENCE
IVY GRAY
LESSIE HARRISON
RONJEANNA HARRIS
SHACRE JONES
CYTEESE ALEXANDER

Moments for Moms II: Peace, Patience, and Balance
Copyright © 2024 by Juanita N. Woodson, Taneshia Yerby, Crystal D. Harrison, Lisa Freeman, Sabrina L. Clemons, Tanisha T. Graves, Sydney E. Scott, Katelyn B. Lewis, Tyresha Baine, Letricia A. Brown, Nikki Lawrence, Ivy Gray, Lessie Harrison, Ronjeanna Harris, Shacre Jones, Cyteese Alexander

Published by Grace 4 Purpose, Publishing Co. LLC

Scripture quotations from The Authorized (King James) Version. Rights in the Authorized Version in the United Kingdom are vested in the Crown. Reproduced by permission of the Crown's patentee, Cambridge University Press

Editing by: Grace 4 Purpose, Publishing Co. LLC
ISBN- 979-8-9908003-2-8
Book Cover Design by: Tucker Publishing House, LLC
Printed and bound in the United States of America

MOMENTS FOR MOMS II: PEACE, PATIENCE, AND BALANCE

Thank you so much to Coach Cathy (Cathy Staton) for your support, diligence and helping to make this project a great success!
I appreciate you tremendously!

MOMENTS FOR MOMS II: PEACE, PATIENCE, AND BALANCE

TABLE OF CONTENTS

DEDICATION

This book is dedicated to every mom, grandmother, or mother figure who has learned to navigate this world and gain peace, patience, and balance in the process. You are an inspiration to other women and appreciated. Keep showing up, we need you.

<u>FOREWORD</u>

Motherhood is a journey marked by joy, challenges, love, and self-discovery. It's a journey that often demands more than it gives (something that many of us didn't expect), yet in those demanding moments lies the opportunity for growth and transformation.

MOMENTS FOR MOMS II: PEACE, PATIENCE, AND BALANCE

"Moments for Moms II: Peace, Patience, and Balance," is more than a book; it's a source of inspiration, and a testament to the strength and resilience of motherhood. Through heartfelt reflections and practical insights from each author, you'll gain a deeper perspective on what it looks like to find peace amidst the beautiful chaos that motherhood sometimes has to offer.

Not only that, you'll come to understand how those small moments of self-care help you to create balance, refill your cup, and find joy in your everyday life.

Needless to say, this book is a must have. The demands of motherhood can knock you down if you let it, and that's why hearing stories from other moms who are (or have been) in your shoes, matters. You are not alone, and a little bit of guidance goes a long way.

MOMENTS FOR MOMS II: PEACE, PATIENCE, AND BALANCE

I'm so thankful that Juanita and her co-authors have created a roadmap to help us all experience more of the joys of motherhood all while caring for ourselves and experiencing real life transformation.

- Taneshia Yerby

Founder of Christian Entrepreneur Org.

MOMENTS FOR MOMS II: PEACE, PATIENCE, AND BALANCE

CONTACT INFORMATION:

Email: info@ceoforwomen.com

Website: www.ceoforwomen.com

Social media: @ceoforwomen

<u>INTRODUCTION</u>

In the whirlwind of motherhood, amidst the balancing acts of responsibilities, joys, and challenges, we often find ourselves yearning for moments of peace, patience, and balance. As mothers, we are the glue that holds our families' worlds together. Constantly juggling roles and aspirations, all while navigating the unpredictable challenges of life. From the tender embrace of newborn cries to the tumultuous tides of the teenage years, and

even learning to parent adult children. Each moment presents its
own set of trials and triumphs.

"Moment for Moms: Peace, Patience, and Balance" is not just a
book; it's a community—a haven where mothers can find
encouragement, and practical wisdom to navigate the ups and
downs of motherhood. Within these pages, you'll go on a journey
of self-discovery, resilience, and growth, guided by the shared
experiences of other mothers and the steadfast presence of faith.

Drawing from personal anecdotes, timeless wisdom, and the
unshakeable foundation of faith, this book is a compass, guiding
you through the storms and still waters of motherhood. Whether
you're a seasoned mom weathering the trials of adolescence or a
new mother tentatively stepping into the unknown, "Moments for

MOMENTS FOR MOMS II: PEACE, PATIENCE, AND BALANCE

Moms" offers hope—a reminder that even in the chaos, there are

moments of peace, patience, and balance waiting to be embraced.

DAY ONE- Crystal D. Harrison

The Journey to Balance Patience and Peace

Motherhood is a profound journey filled with love, joy, and yes, even heartbreaks that can sometimes test the limits of the strongest moms that we know. As mothers we navigate through the sometimes-demanding challenges of caring for our families, our homes, and professional careers. However in today's fast-

MOMENTS FOR MOMS II: PEACE, PATIENCE, AND BALANCE

paced world, where instant gratification and constant stimulation are the norm, the virtues of patience, peace and balance in our lives are often overlooked, even by me. As you will read in this chapter and throughout the pages of this book "Moment's for Mom's" you will discover that these qualities are essential for our everyday well-being and success in both personal and professional realms. I want to explore with you the importance of cultivating patience, peace and ultimately a balance of both in your life daily so that you can experience the full impact of God's unfailing love and purpose in your life each and every day.

Patience is embracing the power of waiting and remaining calm and composed in the face of delays, denials, obstacles, and even the challenges or frustrations of life. I can tell you that many times I have failed the test of patience, but I would challenge each reader that no matter how many times you believe that you have struggled in the area of patience not to give up.

In the book of Romans it encourages us that we must wait patiently for whatever it is that we need or desire to happen. *Romans 8:25 "But if we hope for what we do not yet have, we wait for it patiently."* Patience is in fact a virtue that can help us to navigate through the challenges of life with grace and resilience. Cultivating patience in our lives involves learning to accept things as they are and for me letting go of my immediate need to have instant results when I should allow patience to be at work. *James 1:3-4 "Knowing this, that the trying of your faith worketh patience. But let patience have her perfect work, that ye may be perfect and entire, wanting nothing.* By knitting faith into our lives we have the propensity to minimize stress and improve our relationships. Oftentimes those moments when

MOMENTS FOR MOMS II: PEACE, PATIENCE, AND BALANCE

our patience has been tested we look back and think "darn it wasn't even that serious." One of those moments that stick out in my mind is when my oldest son J.T was two years old. On this particular day I had been at work all day and simply wanted to come home and be able to feed the kiddos, bathe them and read a story but J.T like usual had other plans. J.T decided that after being bathed and dressed he would jump right back into the bathtub fully clothed. Looking as innocent as ever with that J.T charm I had to take a step back from the situation; I had the opportunity to decide if I was going to flip out or just enjoy the moment that my two-year-old decided to have a swim party fully clothed. I decided to enjoy the moment and capture a picture of him in the tub with his blue and white onesies soaking wet. While J.T was not a behavioral challenge, he certainly was not afraid of taking risks as a child; broken arms, stitches, and regular boy injuries more often than most children his age required an extra dose of mom patience.

Galatians 5:22-23 "But the fruit of the spirit is love, joy, peace, forbearance, kindness, goodness, faithfulness, gentleness, and self-control. Against these such things there is no law."

Strategies for cultivating Patience:

1. Create a personal yet private technique that helps you to stay in the moment when your patience is tested or you feel like you have reached your limits of challenges for the moment.

2. Reframe setbacks as opportunities for growth and learning in your life. Setbacks are simply opportunities to grow.

MOMENTS FOR MOMS II: PEACE, PATIENCE, AND BALANCE

3. Set realistic expectations for yourself and avoid over committing yourself.

4. Take a break to reflect when feeling overwhelmed.

A journey towards peace must begin within each of us individually because peace is a choice; a conscious choice that no matter what happens in our lives that we embrace peace. My Pastor Larry B. Surles used to say that "it's not what happens to you but what happens in you." Now he may not have been the originator of that quote, however it has always stuck with me. Our reaction to what occurs can either break our peace or be the bridge to strengthen us while we seek peace. You very well might be saying to yourselves right now that having peace is easier said than done; trust me it can be done.

MOMENTS FOR MOMS II: PEACE, PATIENCE, AND BALANCE

When my children were younger finding peace amidst the school lunches, school PTA meetings, piano lessons, ministry, basketball, football, soccer, tee ball and the occasional chaos just to name a few of our weekly activities seemed to leave no space nor time for peace. I remember driving by Waller Mill Park after picking everyone up from their after-school activities and decided to take the kids to visit the pond that they had. I remember driving in and parking the car; but as everyone hopped out I noticed how quiet and peaceful the park was; It was such a refreshing and calm sound. Once on the bridge above the pond, J.T, Juanita, Jessika, and Robert became so engrossed in the pond that they were constructively occupied for at least forty-five minutes; my thoughts were yippie. "Hey, do you see that mega turtle?" "Do you see the fish?" Do you see the ducks?" This sound was music to my ears, no one was screaming, teasing and J.T and Robert were not saying "stop

17 | Page

touching me." I found my peace at the park right above the pond each day. However, Juanita disrupted my peace at the age of fourteen when she informed me "mom we are too old to be still coming to look at water animals" and "there are bugs out here." Peace will find you as it found me, but when it arrives use it wisely.

As a mother we must be willing to wear multiple hats just to accommodate our children even in the midst of being short on patience and peace at any given time. The saying "happy mom, happy home" is so on point because as mothers we have the propensity to establish the tone in the home and especially with our children. In order to provide a peaceful environment for our families we must be willing to exhibit genuine love for our children. Yes, I know we love our children! But can we love them when they fall short of their own expectations or even your expectations as a parent? Sure you might be disappointed in their decisions in life, but your disappointment and love for your children are two completely separate emotions. When we are able to express those emotions individually we have an opportunity to love our children unconditionally. Matthew 22: 37-39 instructs us to not only love God with all our heart, but it also instructs us to love our neighbor. Guess who our neighbor is? Our children too. I often think of some of the bad choices I have made in life and the one aspect of my failures or shortcomings that will always remain true is that the Father has never removed His love from me.

Setting boundaries with my children, husband and even others outside of our home has helped me to create and maintain a sense of order and peace in my life daily. As a mom, setting boundaries have helped me to prioritize self-care, maintain personal space, and manage expectations that I have for myself as well as those expectations that others might have for me. I must share that practicing self-care is vitally important. Taking care of our own well-being as a mother is essential to be able to nurture our children as well as being able to provide a nurturing environment within the home. Having a support system is important and if I can stress anything, having a support system is ok. We live in a time where most like to announce they did it on their own. Well I never would have made it without Jesus in my life or the great group of women who were busy cheering me on and making the decision not to throw in the towel when I felt weak.

Balancing life is one's ability to maintain a level of stability and harmony in all areas of our lives including work, relationships, families, and our own well-being. Having the ability to juggle

MOMENTS FOR MOMS II: PEACE, PATIENCE, AND BALANCE

these characteristics between various roles and responsibilities has to be very carefully calculated to prevent burnout and frustration.

Peace, patience, and balance are all intertwined qualities that empower us as women, mothers, wives, friends, and professionals to help us navigate life's ups and downs. We can foster a sense of inner patience and peace to withstand challenges with equanimity and lead more balanced and fulfilling lives.

MOMENTS FOR MOMS II: PEACE, PATIENCE, AND BALANCE

Crystal Denise Harrison is truly a woman after God's own heart. She strives to "Raise the Standards" one opportunity, one woman and one purpose at a time in her pursuit to guide other women to discover their purpose and destiny in the Father. Crystal currently resides in Chester, Pennsylvania with her husband Jay of thirty-eight years. Crystal and Jay have seven children ranging in age from thirty-six years old to the youngest

MOMENTS FOR MOMS II: PEACE, PATIENCE, AND BALANCE

who is nineteen years old. Crystal and Jay are the proud grandparents to eight little ones.

Crystal is a graduate of Hampton University where she earned her bachelor's degree in Liberal Arts with a concentration in the ECE field. Crystal continued her education at the University of Phoenix earning a Master Degree in Early Childhood Education.

Crystal is a very involved community leader, mentor, and lifelong educator. Crystal has worked in the ECE profession for more than thirty years. She continues to provide ongoing support and guidance to other ECE professionals and Early Childcare organizations through Circle of Educators and CDH ECE Educational Resources and Services.

MOMENTS FOR MOMS II: PEACE, PATIENCE, AND BALANCE

Crystal is the founder of CDH Ministries and Heart 2 Heart. Heart 2 Heart provides an opportunity to restore the hearts of women one opportunity at a time through mentoring, fellowship, and teaching, so that women can truly experience the love of God's purpose moving in their lives as He created and intended for us to live. Crystal believes that her desire to allow God to use her compassion and purpose in the lives of others will be a guide to many along their journey.

Crystal wrote her first book "How to Fight Fair in Marriage" in 2018 after her marriage was tested and tried. As other tests in her life she fought and won in "in the Ring of Marriage." Her second book "The Traits of Women of Grace" was released in 2023 is a collection of chapters Co-Authored by women who have made a significant deposit in her life over the span of

MOMENTS FOR MOMS II: PEACE, PATIENCE, AND BALANCE

thirty-plus years. "How to Fight Fair in Marriage" and "Traits of Women of Grace" may be purchased on Amazon.

MOMENTS FOR MOMS II: PEACE, PATIENCE, AND BALANCE

CONTACT INFORMATION:

Email: 4cdhministries@gmail.com

Website: www.CDHMinistries.com

Facebook: Crystal Denise Harrison

Heart 2 Heart

Circle of Educators

DAY TWO- Lisa Freeman

Cultivating Inner peace and Boundaries

Hello, my name is Lisa Freeman, this is my second contribution to Moments for Moms and I am elated to share more insight to my perspective on the subject of motherhood. First, I would like to share that at the beautiful age of being fifty-one I have learned to be okay with the fact that some of my prayers are still a work in progress. What I mean by that is this, like some of us,

MOMENTS FOR MOMS II: PEACE, PATIENCE, AND BALANCE

I envisioned the later years of parenting to be somewhat settled, more freedom and the peacefulness of finally being able to sit back and just watch the fruit of my labor. I looked forward to the moments of just being assured that they knew right from wrong, being leaders and not followers. All of the things we teach and preach along the way. However, I have been awakened that there is another tier of motherhood to embrace even when your children become adults. When I think back to how I thought it would be, all I can do is laugh out loud because what was I thinking. There are days that I literally have to shut down and just refocus because if I am not intentional about that my mood for the day would be wrapped around how I am feeling. I have days where I literally just have to tell myself, "no you cannot get involved and they are simply just going to have to be alright." For me it's so imperative that I actually take these moments seriously so mentally I will not crash. However, the way my faith and determination is set up, I have learned to keep me first without feeling guilty. This is not something I have mastered but each day I understand how imperative this is for my mental health. As a mom of adult children, I am still learning to embrace a different level of motherhood. I am finding that I really appreciate who I have become from all of the work put into raising children; which is why I share my thoughts on being okay with setting boundaries for my peace and sanity. Mentally, I had to learn how to release and realign how involved I would be with them becoming adults. Let me share…

Be proud of the work you have put in

I have been a serial entrepreneur for about 29 years. I started my career in 1995 after my daughter was born as a professional hair stylist. I also have two sons, one is married, and the other lives on his own and he is my son who has special needs due to having brain surgery at the age of three. That is another role that requires its own chapter. I give all the glory to God for how he recovered and is still able to live a pretty decent adult lifestyle. As for me there is always decisions to be made on his behalf, paperwork to be filed, and I still have to oversee his daily living. Some of which he often disagrees with because he doesn't quite understand why I still have to oversee his lifestyle. I also own an online fashion boutique, offer personal styling, and I recreate designs. Sometimes I do find myself wondering how do I actually do it all. One because I am doing what I really love so it's not like work for me because I really enjoy what I get to do for a living. The other reason is that I am fully persuaded that, with God all things are possible! (Matthew 19:26 KJV)

MOMENTS FOR MOMS II: PEACE, PATIENCE, AND BALANCE

As I worked diligently building my clientele, throughout the years I worked long hours sometimes into the night. However, I still prioritized my weekends around my children extracurricular, and sport activities. My husband and I even coached some of their sports for years. We were those parents that showed up, popped up and very involved. That was one of the things that I needed to do as a mom because my desire was to be that hands-on involved mom. I wanted them to be active and explore multiple things. So, we made sure we kept them active and we were there to support.

I believe our mission as young parents during their childhood/adolescent years were pretty solid and I have to acknowledge my husband for actually being that example of a father they needed to see. We took our roles seriously because we both came from broken marriages. It was something we agreed upon entering into marriage that we wanted to have a strong bond as parents to be able to parent our family together under one household. We also were committed to modeling that marriage actually works. We wanted them to experience life differently than we did without having to balance life in separate environments. When our parents divorced we both remembered how unsettling it was to have to embrace their new lives, new environments etc.... For me, to live not being able to share both of my parents in one household was sometimes a little overwhelming for me.

So this was an important legacy for me. What about you, do you have a family legacy you know you want to deposit into your family? What does that mean for you? The reason why I asked is because for us it kept us grounded. Marriage has become a thing people enter into lightly. It's one thing to have to manage becoming one but when you decide to add children to the covenant it becomes an even greater responsibility. Our children deserve the best of both a mom and dad regardless of if things work out or not. This is why I had such a sensitive place in my heart when I started my family. I knew I wanted to create change and enjoy having the opportunity to teach & raise my children to live better than me.

As a "daddy's girl" I know first-hand how it feels to have a father as my covering and experiencing his love was one of things that has greatly impacted my life. His love helped me to be confident and courageous because of the way he spoke life into me. He made me believe I could accomplish anything I set my mind to. The conversations we had always made me think and evaluate which led to actually helping me to trust in myself. My mom had ways about her that helped impact the way I take care of myself and how I take care of my home life. She was clearly that mom who helped me take care of my children basically all of their life. I truly believe in the portion of scripture that talks about how older women should be sharing their wisdom to younger women (Titus 2:4-8). Our roles as moms has the ability to change generations and I think that is super powerful. The kind of guidance and love from both of my parents will forever be in my heart. This is why both parents should not take their roles lightly if we really want to create change. The Word of God says that our children are gifts. (Children are a gift from the Lord; they are a reward from him. Psalm 127:3) We should feel honored and highly favored to have been chosen to bring life into the world. We have been given a great opportunity to contribute to the future when it comes to raising our sons and daughters with a shared vision in a loving environment.

MOMENTS FOR MOMS II: PEACE, PATIENCE, AND BALANCE

When we decided to start our family that was one of the first things we agreed upon was to do whatever we needed to do to keep our love alive and our family together. That meant we understood that our lives were no longer just for ourselves. We created time for us and them and we loved each other out loud and in front of them. I think it's important to show children affection and demonstrate how mothers and fathers love each other too. This builds foundation because if we do not lay foundation at home the world will certainly build one for them. We also made sure we enjoyed family times whether it was taking vacations together, experiencing road trips or even just sitting together watching movies and fun videos together.

Along with those good times we also had weekly or biweekly family meetings. They were so helpful because it allowed us more one on one time and to actually hear their points of view of life. During the family meetings we would talk about things we should do next, how things were going, how they felt about certain issues/concerns etc.… This allowed us all to share, vent and laugh out loud. Balancing life and family had its challenges, but for the most part because we had goals and vision, that became a part of our daily commitment. Therefore it helped us to stay grounded which I believe also helped our marriage to continue to grow stronger.

In the midst of being a mother and wife, both roles have truly molded me into the woman I am today. I truly believe that with all of the major decisions, the ups and downs, that I have had to navigate my family through, it has helped me to be a better me. However, there were times when I did not feel equipped to handle some things. My faith had to grow and as I stated earlier I am still navigating my faith to fully trust in God.

MOMENTS FOR MOMS II: PEACE, PATIENCE, AND BALANCE

I feel like there are levels to building your faith. One thing I find consistent is that with each transition gives us the opportunity for growth and that's a good thing. There are times when I even questioned did I do enough now that they are adults knowing good and well I gave my all. These are the b times where I would be overwhelmed from overthinking. You know how we do when we go into the mode of trying to "fix things". They would find themselves in tuff situations and come to me just to vent and I go into problem solving mode. Sometimes you just can't help it because it's natural, you just want to see them winning. Take it from me these moments will always be there you will just have to trust God that they will rely on Him more than you.

Momma's we have to remember to make sure we allow them time to trust the process we preach to others about. If you know you have instilled faith into your children know that they will have their own experiences to trust God with too and some without you. This is the part I had allow myself grace with. Some people call it "letting go". I like to call it "giving myself grace to let go". When your children become of age, leave home, get into relationships, or even get married you are naturally still concerned. Learning how to trust and adjust to this takes time. For some it may take longer than others and that's why I like to say give yourself grace to adjust. Yes we are still their mom but we also have to practice adjusting our input because they have to learn from their own trials and mistakes too.

It doesn't happen as soon as they leave home but over time it is an ever going routine of continued prayers and a routine you have to trust. Every family is different, the way we were raised, our morals, our faith, the way we chose to live our lives are different. You just have to trust the way you have raised yours. Even though they grow into their lives just continue to believe God for wisdom and provision over their thoughts and decisions they may face. Remember all the answers they need may not come from you. Just like with our lives God place certain people in our lives at specific times to assist us. That's why it's always a great idea to sow bountifully and treat people like you want to be treated. A person of good character and consistent in their ways are appreciated. People remember them and will look out for you. This is something I see that shows up for my children. People who value, love & respect me also does the same for my children.

To the momma's who can relate to this, I want to say well done, good and faithful momma! You have done well,

rest assured, you have persevered, you have sacrificed, you have overcome, you are loved, you are appreciated and your labor is not in vain.

To the momma's preparing for this stage, remember what I've shared. Especially the part about giving yourself grace. It's not your job to try and fix everything, God knows all the plans he has for us. (Jeremiah 29:11) Be there to listen and guide along the way. You will always be "Mom" and nobody can ever take that place. Just be prepared to sometimes watch from a distance, your prayers and your presence will always be felt!

Lastly, Live well and maximize the good moments. Prioritize your time as well as setting boundaries. We live happier and more appreciative in balanced environment. We need those moments to just be by ourselves or treat ourselves to a nice evening out, even if it's just taking a ride in the car or to go sit in the park. Enjoy life every chance you get, that means find ways to celebrate even the smallest occasions. Continue to make healthy memories even the ones that try to break you. You were not meant to be broken when you have given your life unselfishly and entirely. You deserve the best too, Enjoy YOU!

If I could leave you with a scripture I have learned to meditate on that has helped me manage my emotions it would be (I can do all things through Christ who strengthens me. Philippians 4:13) When you say it believe it in your heart. Believe that everything you need is already on the inside of you.

MOMENTS FOR MOMS II: PEACE, PATIENCE, AND BALANCE

Who is Lisa Freeman?... She calls herself "A Faith Girl" for it's by faith that she fought for herself, believed in herself, and won victories for herself!

She is a Serial Entrepreneur who began her professional career 29 years ago. She started braiding hair at the age of 13 and later pursued a professional career as a Cosmetologist in her

MOMENTS FOR MOMS II: PEACE, PATIENCE, AND BALANCE

hometown Richmond, VA. In 2002 she moved to Raleigh, NC where she has continued to build her entrepreneurial career.

Lisa is affectionately known as a person of inspiration, self-motivation, and style. Some of her hobbies include family time, DIY projects, shopping, reading, and studying personal development. When asked what's one thing you wished you would have done as a teenager? Her answer was, "I wish I wouldn't have wasted so much time wishing I "fit in" with my peers...I later found out it was preparing me to actually be the change!" When asked, If you could give one success nugget about your entrepreneurial journey what would it be? Her answer was, "To spend every day, several times a day telling yourself, "I can do all things through Christ who strengthens me!" Our words are powerful and using them to speak life over ourselves is the key.

MOMENTS FOR MOMS II: PEACE, PATIENCE, AND BALANCE

Lisa has 3 adult children and 4 grandchildren. She is the owner and creative stylist of an online women's fashion boutique called "Looks by Lisa Freeman" She offers personal styling and she recreates designs. She's an author of her first book "Be the Change" and she has co-authored "Moments for Moms: Volume I and II

Together with her husband "Len" they lead with a life of faith, family, and fun. They have been married 29 years and together 33. They both are advocates in the wellness industry where they assist individuals with maintaining a healthier lifestyle. They also are the founders of a marriage platform called "Marriage That Works" where they provide practical and faith-based advice to couples desiring marriage or needing marital assistance.

MOMENTS FOR MOMS II: PEACE, PATIENCE, AND BALANCE

Lisa also is the Founder of a women's community called "Let's Build Her Up". A platform for women of all ages, backgrounds, and ethnicities to be inspired to fulfill their purpose and passion in life.

Her life's mantra: *Live every day like it's a gift from God!*

You can connect and follow her movement through her website.

MOMENTS FOR MOMS II: PEACE, PATIENCE, AND BALANCE

CONTACT INFORMATION:

www.looksbylisafreeman.com

Email: hello@looksbylisafreeman.com

Facebook: Lisa Freeman

Instagram: thisis_lisafreeman

TikTok: Looksbylisafreeman

DAY THREE – Sabrina L. Clemons
Peace in the Midst of Storms

Being a mother is such a precious gift from God. But let's be

real…sometimes the days are dark, cloudy, and stormy. The

rain falls and the winds blow all while chaos surrounds you.

You long to see the sunlight and at least experience some

moments of peace. You try to escape to a place, at least in your

mind, where you remember the tender thoughts and joy you felt

like the first time you saw your child's face after birth. That is

MOMENTS FOR MOMS II: PEACE, PATIENCE, AND BALANCE

the place where the sun shines, however, life stressors sometimes will cause you to seek solace and maintain your peace, even through the shadow of those memories. Peace is a safe place and everyone needs it in their life.

Life is so unpredictable. Day after day, we have no idea what we may face. Oftentimes, we walk through this journey called motherhood and it can be very chaotic and sometimes very overwhelming. You have multiple responsibilities, wear multiple hats, and everyone needs you. Your children, no matter what age they are, are pulling on you in many different ways. Sometimes even a spouse, loved one, friend too. Your place of employment or business needs your attention. You put on your superwoman hat and try to juggle it all. Most times boundaries are often violated. Then boom, the storm clouds roll in and the

MOMENTS FOR MOMS II: PEACE, PATIENCE, AND BALANCE

bottom drops out and there goes your peace. When this happens, you may feel like you do not have the strength to carry on. However, be encouraged because even in the midst of the storm you can find peace.

Storms come disguised in many different forms. Storms sometimes come to clear pathways. It can cause change in forms. When storms are raging, finding shelter is imperative. Consider embracing the fact that your Heavenly Father is your safe haven from the storm. Understand that He is there to cover and protect in our most chaotic times. Just the thought of this truth brings peace.

In one of many storms in my life, I remember hearing from people who were trying to encourage me, that there is life at the end of the tunnel. However, honestly…I was not seeing it! I was tired, as a matter of fact, exhausted and I felt like giving up. In my early years of marriage, motherhood entered my life. I felt like I was not qualified to be a mother nor did I have the knowledge in my opinion, to do the job well. While I had an eight-month-old, I found out that I was three months pregnant. I remember sitting in the doctor's office in shock and I broke down in tears, crying uncontrollably on my doctor's shoulders. Many thoughts raced through my head.

How in the world was I going to manage two babies? I barely felt I could handle the one. New wife, new mother, new house, and a new job. Lord, HOW? Being a new mom was already challenging. I felt that I needed His help, and I needed His strength right then and there. I knew that the days ahead of me were going to be stressful and complicated. I was really afraid because I felt that I would not have the strength to raise the precious gifts that God was entrusting to me.

I could not do it in my own strength. Not only did I need His super on my natural, but I also needed peace in the midst of what I perceived as a storm. The clouds were dark and I needed to see clearly. Depression started to overtake me. I wanted desperately to be a good mother. I did not think it would be possible to not only find peace in the storm but have tranquil moments once the new baby was born. However, I am happy to say, that's not how my story ended. I had to trust God to cover and guide me. As I did this, eventually I saw the light. It was in these times that my relationship with the Father grew and He caused change in me. I had to hold on to this light through every stage of my children's development. The journey

continues. We may not always understand why things happen in

our lives the way that it does, but there is always a bigger

picture and a greater purpose. Raising those two babies who

were very close in age was not easy. Thus is the experience of

many mothers, whether parenting one or multiples accompanied

with a plethora of duties. I can assure you that with the help of

God and the village He blesses you with, you can do it!

Finding & Cultivating Peace:

Tranquility is serenity. It is a place of being in which inner

peace and calmness prevail. We all need tranquil moments. The

question is how to achieve them. I found that peace

can be found in multiple ways. To cultivate tranquility,

consider implementing the following:

MOMENTS FOR MOMS II: PEACE, PATIENCE, AND BALANCE

1. Give yourself permission to be human – It is okay we are not perfect. Embracing this truth allows us to let God put His super on our natural. His supernatural power gives us strength to persevere. Let go of the weights.

2. See purpose in the storm – Look at the positive versus the negative. Not only does God reveal himself in chaotic times, but he also uses the challenging times to provoke adjustments and growth.

3. Seek peace – Be intentional and chase after peace daily. This is action. Take time to be still – It is in those still small moments that we can hear the still small voice saying, "peace be still." Follow that voice.

4. Keep your mind stayed on Him – The Word says He will keep you in perfect peace whose mind is stayed on Him. Discipline your thoughts.

MOMENTS FOR MOMS II: PEACE, PATIENCE, AND BALANCE

5. Find moments to steal away and rest - Self-care and setting healthy boundaries are essential. This is not a selfish move. Do this without guilt.

6. Learn to trust God in the chaos and in every moment – Trust involves confidence in knowing and believing that He knows all about you and what's ahead. No matter what believe this - He is always there.

7. Meditate – Breathe. Take time out each day to just close your eyes and think about God's word and nurture positive thoughts.

Daily Meditations:

The Lord bless you and keep you; The Lord make his face shine on you and be gracious to you; the Lord turn his face toward you and give you **peace**. (Numbers 6:24-26)

MOMENTS FOR MOMS II: PEACE, PATIENCE, AND BALANCE

As a mother comforts her child, So I will comfort you. (Isaiah 66:13)

The Lord is my strength and shield. I trust him with all my heart. He helps me, and my heart is filled with joy. I burst out in songs of thanksgiving. (Psalm 28:7)

Now the Lord of peace himself give you **peace** always by all means. The Lord be with you all. (2 Thessalonians 3:16)

And the **peace** of God, which passeth all understanding, shall keep your hearts and minds through Christ Jesus. (Philippians 4:7)

Motherhood is not always easy yet so rewarding. It is a gift given from God that brings light into our lives. As a parent, we

MOMENTS FOR MOMS II: PEACE, PATIENCE, AND BALANCE

sometimes experience days in which peace is nowhere to be found, and so does our children, from young to adult.

Nevertheless, finding time to seek and live in peace is necessary to balance our life. Perhaps as you continue on your journey, you will find peace in embracing, meditating, and executing the Father's Word, whom deeply cares for and loves you.

May you be strengthened and encouraged. Even in chaotic moments, just remember the storm will soon past. You got this!

MOMENTS FOR MOMS II: PEACE, PATIENCE, AND BALANCE

Sabrina L. Clemons is a kingdom-minded woman of faith with

a kingdom assignment. Her purpose is to be about her Father's

business bringing glory to Him in everything she does, while

speaking truth in love, life and healing, and the oracles in which

the Father reveals and chooses her to speak. She is a

marketplace leader, serving as a regional director for a nonprofit organization. In addition to being an administrator, Sabrina is an

educator and advocate that works within her community. She

serves on several collaborative teams, taskforces and

coalitions working to end domestic and sexual violence. She is

also the founder of a budding ministry - Rising From the Ashes.

She is dedicated to providing services that stimulates and

enhances growth, development, and solutions for mind, soul &

spirit, while advancing the kingdom agenda. She is determined

to help others experience resurrection power, restoration,

and freedom.

Sabrina L. Clemons is a graduate of Norfolk State University

and continued her graduate studies at Hampton University. She

continues her ministry studies through the Freedom (Life)

School of Ministry and Eagles International Training Institute.

She is a contributing author in the books 'Hear Me Roar' and

MOMENTS FOR MOMS II: PEACE, PATIENCE, AND BALANCE

'The Traits of Women of Grace. Moreover, Sabrina is a woman that loves God first and her family. She is the proud wife of Elder Anthony Clemons and the mother of two beautiful, gifted daughters – Rachel & Sarah.

MOMENTS FOR MOMS II: PEACE, PATIENCE, AND BALANCE

CONTACT INFORMATION:

Email: thekingsagenda12@gmail.com

Facebook: Sabrina Speaks Lyfe

IG: speaklyfe.bri

Website: www.SabrinaLClemons.com

DAY FOUR- Tanisha T. Graves

Girl Don't Lose Yourself When You've Loss a Loved One

When you first conceive, the thought of losing your child never enters your mind. After the pain of childbirth, you experience the joy of looking at their face, smelling their skin, nestling your face against their face, and you fall into a love that you didn't know existed.

MOMENTS FOR MOMS II: PEACE, PATIENCE, AND BALANCE

As you grow with your baby, you never know what lies ahead. Your day-to-day is now different. One minute you are a nurse, the next second a maid; then you turn around and find yourself being a teacher, a motivator, a chauffeur and whatever else that your child is standing in need of. It's during these times that you forget about yourself and attend to being a mother, a supporter, and a listening ear. Being a mother is one of the greatest gifts ever known to woman. God has given you the opportunity to see your child take his or her first walk. To speak their first words, and to hear the name Mama come from their mouth to your ears. Oh! What a joy to hear that innocent voice calling you Mama for the first time.

As your child starts to get older, you pour all that you have into them so that when they get old enough, they will make wise decisions and become a model citizen. But let's just think for a moment, what if your child is not able to care for themselves?

The life of a mother quickly changes and now, you must

prepare for the unknown.

As a Believer, we trust God in all things. That trust is tested

during this time because your baby, your joy, your purpose, is

in a position where you don't know the outcome, and you can

only do so much to help them. Now you must wrap your mind

around the fact that you have to take care of a child who has a

disability. What if you have other children? This changes the

whole dynamic of the household.

This is my story. My son Marquis was born December 12th,

1992. He was diagnosed at five-months-old of being clinically

dead. Imagine my shock and dismay. This is my baby. A

difference in 2-3 minutes could have taken him away from

MOMENTS FOR MOMS II: PEACE, PATIENCE, AND BALANCE

Earth forever. My baby was diagnosed with epilepsy and dealt with it until he took his last breath at the age of 26.

As I begin to wrap my mind around the fact of being a mother to a child who was enduring an illness and having other children to care for as well, I became stressed, strained, and may have even been consumed with depression.

Being a mother, I realized that the lives and the care of all my children were in my hands. So, I did all that I could to be a supportive caregiver to all of my children. They all needed my love, my support, understanding, and encouragement. But, having a child who needed me to be there for his every beck-and-call made life so challenging.

MOMENTS FOR MOMS II: PEACE, PATIENCE, AND BALANCE

I had to find ways to balance being a mom to all of my children, so when he slept I had more time to help my other children with homework or cooking dinner. There were many sleepless nights because of emergency room visits due to Marquis being sick. Those visits didn't stop me from getting up the next morning to send the other children off to school and my husband and I went to work. The love that I had for my children allowed me to push through being overly stressed as I knew that my husband and I needed to provide for the family. There were nights that I had tears falling from my eyes and asking God why He was allowing me and my family to go through so many trials. Overtime, I lost my identity and tried to piece back together the shattered pieces of my life. But the storms kept on raging. There were days that I just wanted to lay around from caregiver burnout because there was no one else around to help.

MOMENTS FOR MOMS II: PEACE, PATIENCE, AND BALANCE

I am here to encourage you that dealing with one child is difficult, but dealing with three requires much patience, and that can only come from God. There are many nights and days that your sick child will need your help. You may have to dress them, bathe them, feed them, take them to appointments, study with them, give medication, and be on guard watching them at all times. This may cause you to lose a good night's rest because you are up and down through the night checking over your child to make sure that they are still breathing. No one can begin to understand your anguish and your need for a Calgon take me away moment. You may even just wish that this time in your life was only a dream. Until that one traumatic day that you awaken and find your child lifeless in bed. You are heartbroken And you gave up your will to live. As a mother you begin to question God, "why, why did you take my baby? I never had a chance to tell him goodbye. I never had a chance to assure him just how much I love him. Father, why, why do I have to endure this pain.?" Then you begin to ask the father to take you on home to glory because your job here is complete. But God reminds you that He is not finished with you yet. God begins to show you that even after loss, you can live again. I am giving you a word of wisdom because I have been there and I am here to remind you that God's grace is sufficient even after death. The loss of life whether it be a child, family member, a friend, your home, your finances; if you keep your eyes on God and know that without a shadow of a doubt, the Lord will redeem you. The burden of loss can weigh you down and they can also cause you to give up allowing the devil to come in to tell you that God has no care for you.

"Nothing takes GOD by surprise, and He using everything for HIS purposes. Now I am sitting at tables that by the world's standards I shouldn't be at. God is using my story to help others. My purpose and calling is great, and so is yours! I ENCOURAGE you to lean on God. Trust in Him for your life journey is in the palm of His hands. He knew you even before you were in your mother's womb. He knew that you would be His. Get up and read the Words of the Lord. Loss can be hard and can cause the believer to question God decision, but know this God knows all, He sits High and looks low. He has not forgotten about you. The purpose that God has over your life shall be completed. There is still beauty followed by a day of sunshine that is given from Our Lord and Saviour Jesus Christ. Mediate on His Word and ask God for guidance in living your life. You will find peace again; death is not the end for you. It is only the plans that God has for you that will last. I want to leave you with my favorite scripture from the King James Bible that read, Philippians 4:13 "I can do all things through Christ that

MOMENTS FOR MOMS II: PEACE, PATIENCE, AND BALANCE

strengthens me." This scripture assures me that I can make it after loss because God will provide me with His comfort, His joy, and His love and He will do the same for you.

I found peace in God as He showed me the life that lies ahead of me. He reminded me that I had a purpose and His plan supersedes my way of thinking. God instructed me to speak about my son and all that we had been through. By doing this, someone else's struggles would become less of a burden. I also found out that my purpose(s) had not yet been fulfilled and I had work to do. The peace of my life had been shattered, but with God I travel the road of Damascus sharing the goodness of God and all that He has done for me.

MOMENTS FOR MOMS II: PEACE, PATIENCE, AND BALANCE

Minister Tanisha Tyler-Graves is a nationally ranked health educator, advocate, and entrepreneur. She educates and bring forth awareness about the stigma that surrounds epilepsy. She spends her time, talent and treasure working alongside vulnerable populations- helping to improve their social, economic and health outcomes.

MOMENTS FOR MOMS II: PEACE, PATIENCE, AND BALANCE

She works closely with various stakeholders including faith-based ministries, veterans, and parents of children with disabilities (e.g., epilepsy, rare diseases, etc....).

She is a sought-after speaker; presenter and panelist. Tanisha is a proud wife, mother, grand-mother and civic leader. She and her husband Bobby work tirelessly to bring focus, voice, and passion to the needs of those who fight for health, economic and social equity, especially those whose voices are left out of the planning tables.

Minister Tyler-Graves is the founder of two nonprofit corporations- "Operation Love Inc". (serving the underserved) and "When The Trumpet Sounds" (advocating for Epilepsy community).

MOMENTS FOR MOMS II: PEACE, PATIENCE, AND BALANCE

Minister Tyler-Graves holds a degree as a Medical Assistant, she also has certifications in Evangelism, and Master's Degree in Biblical counseling. She will be pursuing her Doctorate in Biblical Counseling Sept 2024. She is also a certified seizure and law enforcement instructor. As well as an alumna of F.B.I. Citizens Academy.

Minister Tyler-Graves critiques grants for the federal government as a consumer reviewer for epilepsy, seizures and TBI communities. In this capacity, she oversees studies for potential funding. She has also critiqued medical devices before they are released into the community.

Minister Tyler -Graves has been voted community leader of the year for her service to families. She is also an Ambassador for

MOMENTS FOR MOMS II: PEACE, PATIENCE, AND BALANCE

the Dannydid Foundation and has been highlighted as the ambassador of the month for February and July 2022.

MOMENTS FOR MOMS II: PEACE, PATIENCE, AND BALANCE

Contact Information:

Facebook: Tanisha Graves

Email: wtts4epilepsy@gmail.com,

operationlove2018@gmail.com

Website(s) wtts4epilepsy.org, operationloveinc.org

Tanishatylergraves.com

DAY FIVE-Sydney E. Scott

The Healing Mirror

All too often we are swept into the ebb and flow of life. As moms we know how easy it is to get caught in the storm that we know motherhood to be. This constant balancing act of managing supply and demand, a never-ending list of tasks, appointments, social lives and somewhere in there may be a shower and a spritz of perfume if we are lucky. We have

adopted the "choose your battles" life; because our toddlers will

laugh in our faces if we think otherwise, but somewhere in there

maybe we stopped choosing ourselves. Maybe we even held

onto the battles we didn't choose too tightly and ended up

battling ourselves internally.

Naturally, we tend to shoulder our self-perceived shortcomings

and apply them to our worth and allow it to dictate where we

rank on this unrealistic perfect parent scale, that none of us will

ever come in first place in. Now, before you run too fast with

that last one, let me clarify. There is no rank or place value

when you never stopped winning! Remember those battles I

mentioned, earlier? Remember the ones you didn't choose?

Yes, that was a win for your sanity, and your mental and

emotional health. Shifting perspective!! We must praise

MOMENTS FOR MOMS II: PEACE, PATIENCE, AND
BALANCE

ourselves for what we did do, and not always on what we

didn't! Yes, I see these 50 million Legos on the floor that have

been there since lunch and it is now dinner time, but I chose to

preserve my sanity and this back that's tired of bending and

now I have energy to make this dinner and bake some cookies

as a bonus! Celebrating small victories is just as important as

choosing our battles. Sometimes we don't always know which

battles to choose, and if your brain is as unnecessarily

complicated as mine, trying to figure out which battles to

choose starts an internal WW3. So here are some ways I can

quickly decipher which battles to choose:

1. Is this situation causing harm, or placing anyone in

   danger? Ex. Toddler coloring their whole body in NON-

   toxic marker. No, danger there. Skip it!

2. Is this going to disrupt my inner peace or violate my

   boundaries? Ex. Feeling pressured to show up for an

event, you don't want to attend because you don't have the emotional or mental bandwidth and it takes you away from things you really want and need to do. Nope, cup is empty. Skip it!

3. Will this free me from anxiety, allow me to breathe, make me feel accomplished, or clear my headspace? Ex. Organizing a space in your house, staying home, asking for help, finding support. Oh yeah, that's self-care. Choose it!

4. If it can wait, if you can take it on without it taking from you, if it doesn't dysregulate you mentally, emotionally of physically, and does not disturb your internal or external boundaries, that's homeostasis, that perfect internal balance! If it sounds like peace and feels like peace, CHOOSE IT!

MOMENTS FOR MOMS II: PEACE, PATIENCE, AND BALANCE

On a very ordinary day, I was attending to my daily to-dos when I quickly caught a glance of myself in the mirror. This glance felt different and made me pause. There was nothing different about me, I was in my usual food-stained leggings, overstretched t-shirt, messy bun, and unwashed face; you know, real business casual. Today, it wasn't about how I looked; in that moment I saw myself. I stood in front of this mirror that I so often avoided, as it so loudly reminded me that Newton's Law of Gravity is alive and well. This time, I saw something else. In this moment I stood making eye contact with myself as this montage of my life from childhood to now played like this perfect film. I recalled my traumas, my heart aches, my then perceived failures, my losses, my gains. I was reminded of great shifts I made in my life, moving to a new unknown territory with nothing to my name but an idea, an intention, a purpose. I recalled every single prayer I made, every goal I set, every star I wished on, every journal entry and vision board that I crafted in the name of manifestation. I quickly snapped back to the right here and now and I realized in that moment I had every single thing I asked for and set out to obtain! EVERY SINGLE THING! Despite the forces against me, and being my own opposer at times, or giving in to whatever false beliefs, I never deviated from my objective. Be it depression, anxiety, neurodivergence, being a single mom, unhealed trauma, whatever ailment we encounter, tell me that we don't still find a way through it!

So often we shout out how powerful it is to be a woman, we are phenomenal, we are resilient, mighty, strong, determined, focused, intelligent, and so on, we forget that we are the same women we breathe life into!!! YOU ARE HER! You are that same woman who persisted, who persevered. In fact, I bet if

MOMENTS FOR MOMS II: PEACE, PATIENCE, AND BALANCE

another woman told you your story, you would tell her how amazing or how inspiring she is. We neglect to honor our journeys because life never stops "*lifing*". We forget to look at ourselves and exhale and say, "baby, we made it". Even if we haven't completely fulfilled our goal, I promise if you stop for a moment to befriend and make amends with that mirror to reflect on where you started and where you stand in that moment; you will see that you never ever stopped winning. What is life without skinned knees? We all know scars make for good stories. There are so many obstacles we face as women and as mothers, and we clear hurdles on a daily basis.

We are told to not live in the past and be present in the now, but sometimes we need to visit the past to remind us how rich the present is! When we take time to acknowledge ourselves, and give ourselves our flowers, we will begin to shift our view

MOMENTS FOR MOMS II: PEACE, PATIENCE, AND BALANCE

of ourselves. There is peace in knowing that regardless of any opposing force, you know how to make it happen. Allow this knowledge to fill you to the brim, drink it up! Appreciate every single mirror you have in your home, because now it will forever be your healing mirror that reminded you of who you are! You didn't just survive, you thrived and flourished. We are not our trials and tribulations; we are the big picture! Remember, even artists have to step back from the canvas to see their masterpiece.

Our lives, our journeys, our masterpieces are ever-changing, ever evolving. In the flow of life, we must always remember that we are doing our best. I invite you to practice prioritizing your mental well-being with me. Activate healthy boundaries, pour into yourself, acknowledge what you have done, make time each day to focus on the breath you've been given that fills

MOMENTS FOR MOMS II: PEACE, PATIENCE, AND BALANCE

your lungs with life. Exhale, your doubts and your false narratives that have weighed you down and made you feel less than! You are those inspiring quotes you see and save on the internet. When we keep our cups full, our life directly benefits from the hydration. I know that when I am mentally hydrated/regulated, I notice that my home is peace-filled. My world flows a bit smoother, and I am able to show up wholly. I can already hear you saying, "that its easier said than done". You're not wrong, but you didn't say it was impossible, so let's keep going. How do I do tap into this, on my hard days Syd? Glad you asked! What drives me on even my hard days, to remind me of who I am and where I am going, is my daughters (so cliché'). Stay with me. I not only want my children to flourish as women, but I want them to be mentally healthy and kind women, who fill their own cups, set boundaries, buy themselves flowers, and empower others around them. They are

MOMENTS FOR MOMS II: PEACE, PATIENCE, AND BALANCE

my second mirror and I never want them to avoid the mirrors in their homes, just like I don't want us to. I want us all to look at every mirror we see and give thanks to this perfectly flawed masterpiece. This is an opportunity to renew your inner peace and add patience to your self-care routine. Say it with me, THE PEACE I CREATE STARTS WITH ME, AND MY SUPPLY IS ENOUGH.

MOMENTS FOR MOMS II: PEACE, PATIENCE, AND BALANCE

Sydney Scott worked in the Senior Living and Mental Health Industry, specializing in Administration and Marketing for a collective eight years before becoming a full time stay at home mom. With her immense enjoyment in making human connections and her deep passion to provide a service that brings happiness to others, she chose to become a small

MOMENTS FOR MOMS II: PEACE, PATIENCE, AND BALANCE

business entrepreneur, and capitalize on her love of baking.

Sydney is the owner and operator of Brown Sugar Bake Shop

LLC, where her expertise lies in creating customized

handcrafted cheesecakes. In addition, to being a self-taught

baker, she also is a certified wedding and event planner and is

building her empire of event planning and project management!

Not only is Sydney a business owner and stay at home mother

to three beautiful girls, but she is also a great advocate and ally

to the mental health community. Being an adult who was

diagnosed with ADHD, and being a parent to neurodivergent

children has sparked a new passion within Sydney, and she

actively enjoys connecting with other moms in the

neurodivergent community as well as other business owners

who are navigating through similar experiences. As a result,

Sydney's newest passion project will include a platform where

women can connect and be a soundboard of support through all

MOMENTS FOR MOMS II: PEACE, PATIENCE, AND BALANCE

the lessons life hands us that we just don't talk about enough!

Collectively, Sydney enjoys finding new ways to evolve and connect with other empowered women, raising the next generation of empowered women, and feeding people's souls with her world class cheesecakes.

MOMENTS FOR MOMS II: PEACE, PATIENCE, AND BALANCE

CONTACT INFORMATION

IG: sydventure

Business IG: brownsugarbakeshopllc

FB: Sydney Scott

Email: sydney@brownsugarbakeshopllc.com

DAY SIX- Katelyn B. Lewis
Finding Peace Amidst Chaos

They say it's the joys of motherhood, but life gets hard

sometimes, Mama! It is a journey back to yourself finding peace

learning patience and balancing life while embracing the role of

being a mother.

I had my first son two weeks after my 19th birthday; in all truth

I was still a baby myself. Navigating life and finding balance

MOMENTS FOR MOMS II: PEACE, PATIENCE, AND BALANCE

was of course difficult. Even now as I find time to step away and write this. Creating the time to find those moments for the things that make me, me. Time to write, to sing, to dance, to learn, to relax, or even breathe can be difficult at times but it's still possible. Finding a moment of peace is most important and if all else fails, don't be afraid to hide in the shower!!

Peace can be found in the little moments whether it be reflecting on what has gone right that day or remembering that which is to come. In chaotic times I often think on God's promises to me. That which I know is already on its way to me even if it doesn't feel that way in the moment. There will always be peace in His promises we just have to have patience to wait on the Lord!

Patience is something I've been learning my whole life something my godfather was sure to instill in me. As a child he

MOMENTS FOR MOMS II: PEACE, PATIENCE, AND BALANCE

would always say "Daughter you have to be patient, you gain more when you are patient!" I have to still remind myself of it to this day; patience allows grace, growth, and gain! When we are patient with ourselves, we allow forgiveness and the opportunity to become better. When we are patient with our children, we teach them it is okay to make mistakes while learning, and it encourages them to try again whether it's learning to pour their own juice or learning to ride a bike!

It's not always easy to succeed in the face of adversity and truth be told at times I'd much rather crawl into a ball! But I don't, instead I find my strength in God, family, music, and I get up! Find the things and the people who help you up when you're down. Pray and meditate on your word, reach out to a trusted friend, and place your focus on where you want to be so you can create a plan of action to achieve it. You can do it Mama!

MOMENTS FOR MOMS II: PEACE, PATIENCE, AND BALANCE

Some of the best advice I've ever received came from my godmother. She's a big reason I am who I am today. I used to feel guilty if I ever took a moment for myself because as a young mother, they'll say life ends when you "throw it away" to have children. However, in all honesty my kids are where my life truly began! And even though they are everything; this Mama still needs her moments! My Godmom taught me that taking care of yourself is the best thing you can ever do for your family. Because when we're rested, full and taken care of we can better care for them.

Some of the ways I take care of myself can be as simple as a face mask, glass of wine and rewatching 3 hours of Grey's Anatomy! Sometimes I go to the library with coffee and read a book and if time permits, I'll go for a spa day. But whatever it is, find something you enjoy, something to relax, and recharge

MOMENTS FOR MOMS II: PEACE, PATIENCE, AND BALANCE

because a low battery is never good! (Unless it's on a child's tablet!) We do our best when we feel our best!

When I was in high school, I had an amazing, God filled teacher who always spoke life into me and helped me through so many obstacles. I'd like to say I owe her half of my degree! She'd given me a printout of Mother Teresa's "Do it Anyway" poem; that I kept on the cover of my binder and still have today. It is something I strive to live by and teach to my son's period. Because being forgiving, kind, honest, driven and giving the world goodness even when undeserved is the calling. "You see, in the final analysis, it is between you and God; it was never between you and them anyway." I hope in living and sharing this with my children they will flourish in their purpose and I in my own!

MOMENTS FOR MOMS II: PEACE, PATIENCE, AND BALANCE

Being a mother doesn't come with a manual. Find your moment of peace, have patience, and remember to care for yourself too; with God first, the rest will fall into place.

MOMENTS FOR MOMS II: PEACE, PATIENCE, AND BALANCE

Katelyn B. Saunders is a 25-year-old mother of 3 boys, and she was born and raised in Newport News, Virginia. Katelyn is a singer, songwriter and model featured on various radio stations and playlists across the world under her alias "Kosmic Kae". In addition to her musical success, Katelyn is also an entrepreneur owning her own business & multiple certifications in various fields. She is also adamant about giving back to her community

MOMENTS FOR MOMS II: PEACE, PATIENCE, AND BALANCE

often volunteering with multiple organizations in her area. You can connect with her through social media and support her music on all streaming platforms by searching her album "Forgotten Seeds Still Bloom" by Kosmic Kae.

MOMENTS FOR MOMS II: PEACE, PATIENCE, AND BALANCE

CONTACT INFORMATION

www.KosmicKae.com

Instagram: @officialkosmickae

YouTube: @officialkosmickae

TikTok: @officialkosmickae

DAY SEVEN- Tyresha Nicole Baine

Embracing the Unpredictable Journey

Entering motherhood can feel like losing your identity as you adjust to caring for this new person. It's a profound shift that can leave you feeling like you've lost sight of who you are amidst the demands of nurturing and caring for your child. Yet, in the midst of this transformation, there's also an opportunity for rediscovery—a chance to find yourself again amidst the beautiful chaos of motherhood.

MOMENTS FOR MOMS II: PEACE, PATIENCE, AND BALANCE

The daily life of being a new mom is akin to a new sense of enlightenment, where you become acutely aware of your surroundings and the world around you. With the arrival of your little one, your perspective shifts, and you begin to see things in a different light. Suddenly, you find yourself navigating a delicate balance between caring for your baby, managing household tasks, and tending to your own needs. Each moment becomes precious as you learn to prioritize and allocate your time wisely.

I learned that establishing boundaries is something that has been instrumental in finding balance. For me, it helps me carve out two hours before work to get him fed, bathe & down for a nap. Also setting a schedule on my phone on the days I have to work & important doctor's appointments.

MOMENTS FOR MOMS II: PEACE, PATIENCE, AND BALANCE

Healthy Tips: Prioritize - Knowing what you can handle, and letting go of things that don't need to be done immediately.

Learning to say no - Say no when you need to, and don't feel guilty about doing so.

Manage stress- Managing your own stress is important for you.

In this newfound role, you discover a deep sense of purpose and fulfillment in nurturing and caring for your child. Your days are filled with moments of joy, wonder, and awe as you witness the miracle of life unfolding before your eyes. But along with the joy comes the challenge of finding balance amidst the demands of motherhood. You learn to adapt, to be flexible, and to embrace the ebb and flow of each day. And in the process, you discover a newfound strength and resilience within yourself.

MOMENTS FOR MOMS II: PEACE, PATIENCE, AND BALANCE

As you navigate the ups and downs of parenthood, you find moments of clarity and insight that guide you on this journey of self-discovery and growth. You learn to trust your instincts, to listen to your heart, and to savor the simple pleasures of each day.

Overcoming being impatient within myself was the hardest thing to do for me and that's something I'm still working on daily, feeling like I had to handle things in a hassle manner due to how I was raised. Practicing mindfulness was the best thing I've done. Also being able to be in the present moment, without judging myself. Slowing down was also a huge one to my growth within myself, knowing that my child still loves me regardless of the outcome.

Healthy Tips: Take deep breaths - Count to ten

MOMENTS FOR MOMS II: PEACE, PATIENCE, AND BALANCE

Accept what's out of your control - Knowing you can't control other people's feelings

Yes, the daily life of being a new mom is indeed a new sense of enlightenment—a journey of awakening to the beauty, the challenges, and the endless possibilities that come with the profound gift of motherhood.

Prioritizing mental well-being is very important because in order to raise a child/children you have to put forth the effort to make sure you're okay.

It's important to acknowledge that motherhood is a complex journey with ups and downs, and it's perfectly normal to experience a wide range of emotions along the way. While there may be moments of calm and tranquility, there can also be moments of intense stress, uncertainty, and even chaos. In the

MOMENTS FOR MOMS II: PEACE, PATIENCE, AND BALANCE

moments of stress or even uncertainty I turn on my favorite music, it seems as if music helps you release a different ease. I secondly calling on the man upstairs because in the end you can't do nothing without him.

Healthy Tip: Music can be incredibly therapeutic, and finding solace in faith and spirituality can provide strength and support during challenging times. It's good to find different practices that bring you comfort and help you navigate the ups and downs of motherhood. Remember to be patient with not just your children/child but also yourself as you navigate the complexities of motherhood.

Being a new mother with anxiety made me feel like I had to do things in a hastily manner, causing me to be overwhelmed and finding myself frustrated crying while caring for my son.

MOMENTS FOR MOMS II: PEACE, PATIENCE, AND BALANCE

Everyday wasn't as easy but as time went on I would remind myself that regardless my son still loved me. In motherhood it's okay to have difficult days or moments where things don't go as planned. What matters most is the love, care, and presence you provide for your child, even amidst the challenges. Having Patience within yourself and your child saves you from feeling like things have to be done in a hastily manner and beating yourself up because things couldn't get done that day.

 Practicing Self-Compassion is to remind yourself that it's normal to have doubts and feel exhausted sometimes. Treat yourself with the same kindness and understanding that you would offer to a friend in a similar situation. I'm somebody that I needed at my youthful age to my son, knowing that at the end of the day my son needs me more than anything. I wake up telling myself I can do it with tears in my eyes. Never hesitate to ask for help because you're not alone.

MOMENTS FOR MOMS II: PEACE, PATIENCE, AND BALANCE

GOD IS WITHIN HER SHE WILL NOT FALL
(Psalm 46:5)

Being a new mother I truly had to learn that it was okay to need time to myself and to take breaks even if it isn't nothing but 5 mins of me going outside to just breathe.

It's extremely important to find a self- care routine. Did you know that the quality of the mothers well-being affects the child the most? Take care of yourself, both physically and emotionally. This could mean taking short breaks when needed, getting enough rest, eating well, and engaging in activities that help you relax and recharge. I recharge by sleeping when he's asleep, stepping out of the room and coming back when he's awake. If you have a mental health condition like me then it's extremely important to take time for yourself after caring for your child/children because you don't want to become overstimulated. When you contribute to yourself, you make yourself more available to your child's every need while feeling good doing it.

Here's my advice to any new mother: Don't allow anybody to make you feel any type of way about how you're raising your child. Stop setting unrealistic expectations for yourself, know that you cannot do it all. Some things will take more time.

MOMENTS FOR MOMS II: PEACE, PATIENCE, AND BALANCE

Tyresha Nicole is a First-Time Author, First-Time Mother,

Patient Service Advocate for the elderly, and generational curse

Breaker. Tyresha has spoken at Various events and is also the

Founder/CEO of Girls United 4 Life mentoring program

MOMENTS FOR MOMS II: PEACE, PATIENCE, AND BALANCE

dedicated to helping at-risk youth. Tyresha's dedicated to breaking generational curses and empowering others.

MOMENTS FOR MOMS II: PEACE, PATIENCE, AND BALANCE

CONTACT INFORMATION

Email: Tyreshanicole3@gmail.com
Facebook: Tyresha Baine
Instagram: Iamdopechic
TikTok: Tyreshanic

DAY EIGHT- Letricia A. Brown
The Balancing Act

The day is warm, and excitement is in the air! We've been preparing for Family and Friends' Day. My belly is as large as a basketball, and that was large for my 4'11 small frame. The year was 1985, I was nine months and counting, and trust me, the "wobble" was real. I couldn't see my feet and my back felt as if it would snap in two.

MOMENTS FOR MOMS II: PEACE, PATIENCE, AND BALANCE

Nevertheless, everything was prepared in order and ready...

including the bundle I carried...ready or not, here he came. A

beautiful bouncing baby boy, weighing in at 6lb and 12oz,

healthy and absolutely adorable! Even my Doctor was elated.

Sad to say, I didn't make the Family and Friends' Day.

I shared this portion of my days of early motherhood, to shed a

little light on the "Balance" of Life. Unfortunately, life does not

necessarily tick to our clock nor send off an alarm when danger

is present. Who or what can prepare us for life's challenges of

motherhood? My answer, only God!

God truly amazes me in the fact that, He came to earth as a

babe. Included in His own plan...Yes! He planned His own life,

death and resurrection! Mary had been chosen to carry the

prophecy in her very womb. She was a virgin untouched by

MOMENTS FOR MOMS II: PEACE, PATIENCE, AND BALANCE

man...overshadowed by the Holy Ghost and conception began...upon her...the Balance of Life began on earth. Although foretold, nothing and no one could've prepared her for the agony, despair, hurt, disappointment, and grief she would experience as a young mom. What will give us the fortitude, will-power, energy, and sheer tenacity to endure and press pass the pain life dishes us? Only Gods' love, healing, and strength!

The struggles of a single mom family home, or the bliss of a husband lead, family home, there has to be balance. Life deals what it deals, however we have been created to problem-solve, maneuver through foreseen and unseen obstacles, to dismantle illusions, build, support, and bring balance, to the family structure.

MOMENTS FOR MOMS II: PEACE, PATIENCE, AND BALANCE

What is balance? Let's ask the very thing that was entrusted to us, the revelation that we're fearfully and wonderfully made! We truly are. We've been created, formed, and fashioned in God's mind before the foundations of the world began. As stated before we've been fearfully and wonderfully made by God.

The uniqueness of our body structure is miraculous to say the least. There is a center with identical extremities on each side; one-head, one-heart, one-stomach, one-liver and one mouth. One-brain with two sides, two- kidneys, two-lungs, Two-hands, five-fingers (on each hand), and five toes on each foot.

The human anatomy and it's complexities depicts the mind of God. The heart being the center and serving as the anchor point of balance. We are to remain undivided, in mind, body,

soul and sprit, how does one balance it all out?

My mother use to say, "too much of anything will bring

turmoil." As we go about this life, God Himself must be the

focal point. The Word says that He's the Mediator, that means

He is one who stands in the middle. It is safe to say that if we're

going to maneuver through the canals of life, we must stay

centered in Christ. In all your ways acknowledge Him, and He

shall direct your paths. He has given us a line-up:

GOD

FAMILY

EVERYTHING ELSE

He Himself has designed us in balance, and with Him being the

center, there is no room for Teeter-tottering or being off

balance. As a child there were toys that weebles-wobble but they don't fall down.

Balance can be found if we learn from our mistakes, re-arrange our priorities, regulate, and re-calibrate the situations we find ourselves in. Walking in healing and wholeness from any illness will more than likely reflect an imbalance in diet and exercise. God has provided us with everything we need to maintain our physical system and it is capable of processing through our brain and other organs in order for our equilibrium to keep us in balance. Our overall health and well-being is predicated on being and remaining in balance.

Vertigo is a condition that causes an off-balance in the body. We must also beware of what I named.... Spiritual vertigo, even in Ministry and pouring into others an imbalance can occur.

MOMENTS FOR MOMS II: PEACE, PATIENCE, AND BALANCE

The Balance Act

It is not required that "you" balance everything, but rather you yourself be in Balance. When you are in balance with God's will – He will in turn work all thing together for your good.

Let's leave the acrobatics and walking the tight rope to the Circus. We will leave walking the balance beam to the Olympics. But we shall live, move, breathe, and have our being in Him! We have grace for balance already built in! All we need is within us! Just walk in obedience and in it!

The dedication to my heavenly Father supersedes even my own belief. He graced my life with His presence, and I desired Him more than life itself. I vowed that no man would touch me until I was his wife; nine years between my oldest and my middle son proved that my heart was true. No amount of preparation could possibly prepare me for what I was about to encounter.

I remember the night my second son was conceived, and Abba told me that He had blessed my womb. I saw the sweetest, cutesiest little boy, with a smile that could melt the hardest frozen ice-cream and light up the darkest room, I felt in my heart that he was an angel on loan. I knew that he'd never give me a daughter-in-love, or baby grands (not talking about biscuits here, smile), but his time on earth would be short naturally not wanting to check on that, I pushed it to the back of my mind.

The year is 2005, I'd been Nominated for a lifetime Achievement Award at the Convention Center in Norfolk, VA.

MOMENTS FOR MOMS II: PEACE, PATIENCE, AND BALANCE

God spoke clearly and said, "welcome to the next level." My question was what is this going to cost me? He said, "Do you love me." My answer was yes. He asked, "Do you trust me?" My answer was, yes! Lord I trust you. He then asked, "Finally, do you believe in me!" By then, tears fell and I was shaken. Three days later at midnight my phone rang. It was my son's girlfriend, saying that he'd been in an accident, and he didn't make it, as she went ballistic screaming on the phone, I stood frozen in place. I'd awakened out of sleep thirty minutes prior. My body functions lost composer, and I had to change and shower, (it was at that moment, that my middle son had transitioned). After, hanging up with her, knees buckle and I did the only thing I know for sure how to do, and that was to pray and talk to God. He showed me an open vision, and Ray stood talking with the Angel. The conversation went on this way:

MOMENTS FOR MOMS II: PEACE, PATIENCE, AND BALANCE

Ray: But what about my Mom?

Angel: Your Mother will be fine.

Ray: But I want her to be happy.

Angel: She will be fine.

And God said to me," If he stays alive, he will be paralyzed from the neck down, there would be no quality of life, and he won't be doing what he loves (he played basketball full scholarship with Northrop Grumman-NNSB)." All of that to him would be death. So I understood that God would let him stay, but his body would be broken. Ray Jr. knew that I would cancel my entire life and ministry to take care of him. I was told by my Heavenly Father that I had to do his Eulogy….. and so I did. During this time, I totally poured into my two sons all the love and support I could muster. The knowledge I have now certainly would have helped in the healing process, and I definitely would have sought external counsel for us all.

Many of his peers gave their hearts to Christ (15 to be exact) and now have families, businesses, and yet living wholesome lives for God. Family is most important to God the Father. I am reminded, that absent from the body is present with the Lord. Ray knew and was prepared by a dream he'd had…..but that's another story. We must make sure that we let those we love know that we indeed love them. Tomorrow is not promised, nor is it certainty of life, ministry, social life, and such. We must distribute our love, time, energy, support, as well as attributes, personal desires equally, proportion evenly, to prevent aspiration and falling off balance. Sometimes no-is in order! That's a Big One! God Himself is our stabilize and you yourself alone, cannot be all things to all people…. only God the Father

MOMENTS FOR MOMS II: PEACE, PATIENCE, AND BALANCE

is- Omnipresent and Omnipotent. So, remember; not too little, not too much But Just Right!

Helpful Tools and Suggestions:

Prayer First and Foremost

Planners/Journals

Vision Boards/Vitamins regiment

Quiet Spaces/Home/Library/Beaches

Home Cozy Corner

Meal Plan

Counseling (if necessary)

Self-Care/relaxation

Hobbies

Exercise class

Community outreach/activities

No social media zone

MOMENTS FOR MOMS II: PEACE, PATIENCE, AND BALANCE

Biblical References

Matthew 1:16-24

Matthew 2:3

John 1:29-34

Isaiah 7:14

Isaiah 53

Psalms 139

Romans 8:28

Apostle Dr. Letricia A. King Brown D.Th.
K.I.N.G.D.O.M International Ministries
K.I.N.G.D.O.M Ministries Church
Visionary, Founder, Senior Pastor

A native of Pascagoula, MS, Apostle King Brown is the mother of three sons, Dante, Rollen Jr. (present with the Lord), and Joshua. She is also has three beautiful granddaughters and three handsome grandsons. She is the visionary and founder of

MOMENTS FOR MOMS II: PEACE, PATIENCE, AND BALANCE

Kingdom Ministries Church, which was birthed September 2000 and serves as Senior Pastor in Newport News, Virginia.

Apostle Letricia Brown gave her life to the Lord March 15, 1982, and God has proven the fruit of her labor. Chosen by God and called to the Five-Fold-Ministry in June 1983. Apostle has an awesome mantel of prophetic anointing, the fruit, and gifts of the Spirit in operation, healing and deliverance ministry manifested. She has faithfully served in various capacities in ministry. She holds a Diploma in Executive Secretarial and Business Administration and has held a position as a schoolteacher in the Newport News, Virginia school district. Apostle attended Apostolic International Theological University, Duluth Georgia where she received a Doctorate in Theology. Dr. Brown is the President of Kingdom International Theological University in Newport News, Virginia. In the fall

MOMENTS FOR MOMS II: PEACE, PATIENCE, AND
BALANCE

of 2020 the newly released Kingdom Living Magazine was

published. The unveiling of Kingdom Global Alliance Network

(KGAL) was launched October 2021.

Dr. Brown is also an entrepreneur, visionary and founder of

Handmaidens of Excellence Ministry. Apostle a published

author of "The World of Four" Series (Children's Book) and

"Apostle's Inspirational Quotes". November 1, 2022, Apostle

Brown signed a contract on her very first business venture

"La'She Boutique.

God had a greater vision with the birthing of K.I.N.G.D.O.M.

International Ministries Inc, which serves as a covering and

birthing of new ministries global. Kingdom Ministries Church,

Newport News, VA, Ambassadors for Christ Worship Center,

MOMENTS FOR MOMS II: PEACE, PATIENCE, AND BALANCE

Petersburg, VA, Harvest Ministries, Waldorf, MD and Lifeline Outreach Deliverance Center, Philadelphia, PA.

Committed to the task that God has put before her not by letter, but by experience she has been tried by fire and has come forth as pure gold. Apostle has traveled to Senegal West Africa, Mexico and the Bahamas as a missionary helping hurting hearts suffering and those who are without Christ. Her desire is to see the body of Christ come together in unity, maturity and grow in love.

The scripture that truly portrays her life is found in Philippians 3:7-10. "All that I have attained: I count as loss; for the excellence of the knowledge of my Lord Jesus for whom, I have suffered the loss of all things; and count them rubbish, that I

MOMENTS FOR MOMS II: PEACE, PATIENCE, AND
BALANCE

may gain Christ; and found in Him, not having my own

righteousness, which is from the law; but that which is

through faith in Christ. That I might know Him, and the power

resurrection, and the fellowship of His suffering, being

conformed by His death." Yet, I press on!

MOMENTS FOR MOMS II: PEACE, PATIENCE, AND BALANCE

CONTACT INFORMATION:

Email: letriciakingbrown@gmail.com

Facebook: Apostle Letricia Brown Ministries

Facebook: Kingdom Ministry Church

Facebook: Handmaidens of Excellence

www.Kingdom-Ministry.org

Email: Kingdomintlministries@yahoo.com

Phone: 1-833-9KINGDOM 1 (833) 954-6436)

DAY NINE- Nikki Lawrence
Daily Sips of Tea

Patience - Requires Lipton Lemon Tea, Hot with a hall's mint to chill any possible attitude.

Patience according to Webster's Dictionary is defined as the capacity to accept or tolerate delay, trouble, or suffering without getting angry or upset. What a thought as a 41-year-old mother. Now, as I have finally accomplished things, I think back to when I was 19. Young, married and accepting the birth of a child! Oh! The excitement of new life .. but the thought of not knowing if I could tolerate the thing growing inside of me for the next nine months, not knowing that it would delay the progress of my future education and career experiences, not knowing the amount of suffering I would experience and the strength that only God would give to me to never truly be upset. Is this real?? Patience is so overpowering and forgiving it can sometimes be blind to its own error of love. The love that overshadows wrongdoing and shelters us from the pain of the world. God has strengthened me to deal with these moments slowly. First, He told me, "Be at "Peace," you did your job"!

Peace- Requires Peppermint Tea with a Peppermint Stick Hot to wake up any senses and motivate the mind.

MOMENTS FOR MOMS II: PEACE, PATIENCE, AND BALANCE

Peace- As a mom. Peace is so mundane it comes and goes in spurts. It's like the sun, you know it's going to come up and go down. Peace was a thing of the past when I was a young mother. I was so tired all the time and I didn't know where it was coming from, who would provide it, or who had the power source for peace. What did it look like? I think in my younger years I went through a woe-is-me phase with peace. I was praying all the time, "God I see mothers out her striving, and making big things seem small while my small things seem big. I can't even get out of bed in the morning, I can't control my emotions, I don't know if by having kids I missed out on an opportunity or if I'm missing out on an opportunity but not experiencing the joys of having kids because all I see is work". My younger self as a mom spent so many hours just trying to put the puzzle together, like what are these other moms doing that I'm not doing right?? And I finally figured it out. They

MOMENTS FOR MOMS II: PEACE, PATIENCE, AND BALANCE

weren't wearing their struggle every day, or walking around as if the world was ending because it wasn't. It was so dramatic. God literally answered my prayer as soon as I prayed it again. God gave me joy, peace and understanding. Now I just needed to balance it. I needed to balance my emotions between the frustration of cleaning all the time and cooking all the time. It was a lesson of, who and what are you raising this little person to become? Are you offering peace in the home or the world's problems? Was I being a role model for these two little bodies that I created or a dictator? Once I began questioning those aspects of my life I began to change the way I looked at those moms that I personally thought were so great but not in judgment but in a way of how can we have playdates with our kids, I want my girls smiling more because when they have peace I have peace and that means our life will start to flow differently and look differently. All I needed to know was how to balance it so that I would be effective in the future.

Balance-Peach Tea with a little shot of Lemonade and mint Cold to reflect on the wonderful Job you have done.

Balance- How do you balance an act? Or what seems to be an act? At first, you have conquered patience and peace, but when you learn to balance it out, it becomes an act or what you want the world to see vs what is really going on. Dressing the same and cooking dinner every day at 5pm is a representation of what you want your kids to see. So, you are balancing. Changing the way you speak so that your children learn a different diction than you; you are balancing. Not choosing to be above others, just choosing different for your children and even yourself in some aspect. However, it takes a while to grasp the reality that

MOMENTS FOR MOMS II: PEACE, PATIENCE, AND BALANCE

everyone is not perfect and will not be perfect. It takes a while to get over the fact that you put in all that hard work changing you for them just to find out you didn't raise angels, as much as you sheltered them and loved them. *OUR KIDS WILL MAKE THEIR OWN CHOICES,* and it's no reflection on our parenting, it's a reflection on the world changing and growing and our children having to adapt. Compare our 1993 to their 2024, we have done amazing! And we must give ourselves credit. We balanced through Covid, the K2 drugs, kids dropping in and out of school, school shootings and unemployment. Some marriages didn't make it but, us moms, we did and so did our babies.

We balanced through good and bad times, ups and down and we did it all with God and a Good glass of Tea. Anything is possible!

MOMENTS FOR MOMS II: PEACE, PATIENCE, AND BALANCE

Dr. Nikki Lawrence, born and raised in Williamsburg, VA., is a mother of four (2 Bonus kids) and the love of one, Adolph Smith.

Dr. Lawrence has a passion for writing, HR work and working with youth and adults suffering with mental health crises/ disorders. Which is why she started along with a close friend a mentoring group called "Pearls with a Promise" and her new counseling firm "Speaks Volumes" to continue her mission in advocating for the voices of our next generation which she passionately refers to as the "Generation of now".

Dr. Lawrence also has a podcast called, "What Happens in the Bedroom", where she and her co-host Brenda Harris, discuss some of the issues today. Issues in marriage, friendships, church, with youth and even the workplace. Their podcast can be streamed on Spotify podcast.

Dr. Lawrence also believes with" God and a good glass Tea anything is possible".

MOMENTS FOR MOMS II: PEACE, PATIENCE, AND BALANCE

CONTACT INFORMATION:

Facebook: Nikki Lawrence

Website: https://speaksvolumes.my.canva.site/counselingfirm

IG: speaksvolumescounselingfirm

Email: speaksvolumeslh@yahoo.com

DAY TEN- IVY GRAY

Relay on Resilience

My name is Ivy. I am many things to myself and the people in my life that depend on me: intimately, professionally or as our lives cross temporarily. The person who depends on me most to teach her who she is, who she could be and to see her through the journey of becoming is my 12-year-old daughter Micah. I have learned so many things about myself as a woman just from being a mother to a daughter. I am constantly learning new things about Micah as she changes in style, emotions and physically. I have a front row, center seat in the stages of her childhood and development. I will soon be a mother to another little girl, who is now developing in my womb, equipping herself for arrival and to join our loving family. We patiently await her. We already love her. I have asked God why He wants me to be a mother to girls. A mother to girls requires me to be sure of myself as a woman. It demands my self-esteem and self-worth to be intact. I am the most influential example to my daughters and I feel burdened to do right by them.

Resilience

There may have been a time or two that you've told yourself that you're not as good of a mom as you'd like to be. You may have even thought that you could be doing a disservice to your children because of the areas in which you lack. No mother is perfect and some of these self-accusations may be true. I have

contemplated these concerns for years. Like you, there have

been times in my life where I was simply just too busy. Busy

providing to maintain the bare necessities when I was a single

mother. Away from home too often as a working mother. Busy

healing when I was a depressed mother. Having to choose

homework over play time as a studious mother. Sacrifice was

the name of the game but similarly to other lifelong

relationships, your relationship with your children goes through

waves and phases. Motherhood is a lifelong undertaking, and

the secret to its success is resilience.

Resilience is a type of strength that enables you to

recover from any form of difficulty. A natural endurance and

self-motivation that nudges you when you fall and reminds you

to get back up and try again. This to me is one of the most

MOMENTS FOR MOMS II: PEACE, PATIENCE, AND BALANCE

important tools of parenting. Despite the sacrifice, setback, or detour, take strength in knowing that you can always try again. While some things cannot be undone, they can be redone.

Here is a piece of my story: It has always been my lifelong goal to go to a university level college and gain an honorable degree. I did not accomplish this goal before my daughter Micah was born. I had the time, and the opportunity but throughout the years life's distractions and setbacks got in the way. Honestly speaking most of our setbacks and distractions are of our own doing resulting from poor choices and bad decisions but you and I have to self-examine and take accountability for those things through self-reflection. Self-reflection is not meant for you to condemn or punish yourself. It's also not meant for you to take on so much self-pity that it consumes you and it's most definitely not designed to allow you to make excuses. The purpose of self-reflection is to help you to get to the root of the

MOMENTS FOR MOMS II: PEACE, PATIENCE, AND BALANCE

pattern of your mistakes, learn and grow from them and move forward.

Sixteen years have passed since my pursuit of higher education and twelve years have passed since becoming a mother. Throughout those years I've taken a few classes here and there at several different community colleges across the states where I have lived. I even finished a nursing program as a licensed practical nurse. Only now have I made it to university level education as a sophomore in college. What got me here and what will get you where you desire to be is resilience. "I'm always falling forward" is a phrase that I use very often. Which simply means to continue to make progress even while failing. Whatever the task may be win or lose, victory or defeat, discover the ways in which you have made progress. Find out

what progression looks like for you but here are a few strategies
that can help.

1. **Be empowered by your mistakes but don't let your
   mistakes overpower you.** In other words, don't dwell
   on the mistake made, instead acknowledge it and shift
   your focus on what you've learned from it. As a mother
   you will get it wrong every now and then but what you
   learn from the wrong adds to wisdom.

2. **Reassign guilt.** You are a busy mother. Indeed! But
   you are not just a mother, you're also a woman, wife,
   student, coworker, employee, boss, friend, club member;
   an endless partaker of many things. Be honest with your
   children about how you will share your time between
   them and the other responsibilities that you have.

3. **Make a plan** and allow your children to be a part of it.
   Throughout my career and education pursuits, I have

always made a plan on how I'd maneuver through each

task. The plan would have a start date and end. A why

and desired outcomes. Next, I'd take that plan to my

daughter and go over it with her and ask how she'd like

to be included and how she felt about the process as it

would impact her life along with mine.

4. **Don't give up.** This sounds like something you hear as a

blanket statement of encouragement to fit any mold.

However, this is the ultimate requirement for all things

that lead to success. It takes time (and resilience), allow

yourself the peace in knowing that it may not happen

overnight until the one night that it does.

Along with the pursuit of self while being a mother is

the resilience required in the pursuit of parenting. You will

experience tough times with your children at each phase of their

MOMENTS FOR MOMS II: PEACE, PATIENCE, AND BALANCE

childhood from keeping them safe as a newborn and toddler, to teaching responsibility, self, and body image as a preteen and teen. I have not reached the college years in experience with my own daughter but I can expect that could be tough as well.

The best way that I have found to navigate through these stages of parenting and childhood is honesty. Firstly honesty with yourself then honesty with your children and your support system.

Mother: **Honestly**, I do not like how much my infant cries, it can be overbearing.

Mother: **Honestly,** my toddler does not listen and that frustrates me.

Mother: **Honestly**, raising a preteen/teenager is hard, she's right, I can't always relate to her and her feelings, it's been too long since I've felt what she's going through.

MOMENTS FOR MOMS II: PEACE, PATIENCE, AND BALANCE

I find that when I am honest with my daughter about how I'm feeling, with respect to her age and what's appropriate for her to know, it releases some of my anxiety and the negative feelings that may be associated with the issue. It also contributes greatly to my mental health. Being honest with my support system when I need help, a break or just a moment to myself allows me to regroup and return as a better mother. Just as importantly, allowing my daughter to be honest with her thoughts, feelings, desires and critiques both good and bad keeps her mental health and internal self-reflection intact. A bond of trust is needed in each stage of life together and to me, this is the best way it is achieved.

As you already know very well, you cannot plan and predict all of life's experiences, but you can continue to sharpen your mind to always get up after a fall and start again after a setback. Along the journey you and your children will gain endurance, mental fortitude, and a bond that is not easily

broken.

MOMENTS FOR MOMS II: PEACE, PATIENCE, AND BALANCE

Ivy Gray is the author of other books in the genre of self-improvement and development. Ivy is pursuing a specialty in the study of mental health with the belief that "life first happens in the mind and is lived out by choices, and decisions made based on circumstances and situations that are presented to us that may or may not be in our control." She is a devoted, happy

MOMENTS FOR MOMS II: PEACE, PATIENCE, AND BALANCE

wife and an ever-evolving mother of two daughters. A poetic author and novelist.

"Most of all I desire to use words to bring to life the thoughts and feelings of my readers, peers, those who feel unheard."

MOMENTS FOR MOMS II: PEACE, PATIENCE, AND BALANCE

CONTACT INFORMATION:

Website: www.toowhomitmaydesire.com

Email: toowhomitdesires@gmail.com

Facebook: Ivy Gray

Instagram: olori_ivy

DAY ELEVEN- LESSIE HARRISON

Finding Peace in the Promise: Trusting. God Through Life's Storms

Throughout my life, one scripture has resonated with me more than any other is John 14:1 "*Let not your heart be troubled: ye believe in God, believe also in me.*" These words spoken by Jesus have been a source of comfort and strength for me in the face of life's challenges. In this scripture, Jesus is really reminding us that no matter what if we put our complete trust in

MOMENTS FOR MOMS II: PEACE, PATIENCE, AND BALANCE

the Father there will be a place of refuge when the storms of life exhaust us. "Do not let your hearts be troubled. You believe in God; believe also in me." These simple yet powerful words remind me that no matter what storms may come my way, I can find peace in the presence of God.

As a mother of four children, life has presented me with its fair share of trials and tribulations. From sleepless nights and endless worries to moments of joy and laughter, being a mother has been both a blessing and a challenge. Through it all, I have found peace in knowing that God is with me every step of the way.

Jesus' promise of peace to those who believe and trust in Him has been a guiding light in my life since I can remember and that trust has only grown over the years. In moments of doubt and fear, I have turned to Him in prayer, seeking His guidance

and comfort. And time and time again, I have experienced the

peace that surpasses all understanding, a peace that can only

come from God. **Philippians 4:7** *"Let not your heart be*

troubled: ye believe in God, believe also in me."

Now, at the age of eighty-three, I look back on a life filled with

ups and downs, trials and triumphs. Through it all, I have seen

God work miracles in ways I could never have imagined. His

faithfulness and love have sustained me through some of the

darkest of days and brought light and hope into my life that has

been everlasting.

One of the most important lessons I have learned on this

journey is the importance of prioritizing my time and energy to

help me maintain balance within my household. Early on, I

realized that my own abilities have limitations, but with God by my side, all things are possible. By putting my trust in Him and seeking His will above all else, I have found peace and purpose in every season of life..

As I reflect on the words of Jesus in John 14:1, I am reminded that no matter what circumstances may come my way, I can rest in the knowledge that God is with me. His promise of peace is one that I hold onto tightly, knowing that in Him, I will find strength, courage, and hope for the journey ahead. May we all take comfort in the words of Jesus and trust in His unfailing love, knowing that with Him, we can face each day with confidence and peace in our hearts.

As a mother, widow, and caregiver, my life has been a journey of faith, perseverance, and learning to lean on the strength of the

MOMENTS FOR MOMS II: PEACE, PATIENCE, AND BALANCE

Father above. After the passing of my beloved husband, James L Harrison, I found solace and moments of reflection in caring for my children and feeding the community. Motherhood has been my greatest blessing, and through the challenges and triumphs, I have found opportunities for reflection and peace with God, my safe haven of restoration and peace.

In the midst of the chaos of daily life, I have learned that stepping back and finding time to be alone with the Father is essential for maintaining my sense of self and patience. It is in these quiet moments that I realign myself with the values and virtues that the Lord has instilled in me. I have come to realize that straying from my boundaries can lead to impatience and uncharacteristic behavior, which is not the person God intended me to be for my family and loved ones.

MOMENTS FOR MOMS II: PEACE, PATIENCE, AND BALANCE

In times of overwhelming challenges, I have discovered the power of prayer and walking away from a situation to regain perspective. Instead of giving in to the impulse to react impulsively or harshly, I choose to retreat, pray, and allow for a cooling-off period. This practice has become a valuable tool in my arsenal of patience, enabling me to approach situations with a clear mind and a calm spirit.

My journey as a mother to four unique children has taught me the importance of recognizing when I need help and when to seek guidance from the Lord. Each of my children possesses their own distinct personalities, requiring tailored approaches and, at times, divine intervention. There have been moments of doubt and exhaustion when I have had to acknowledge my limitations and simply rest, trusting that God will provide the strength I need to carry on.

MOMENTS FOR MOMS II: PEACE, PATIENCE, AND BALANCE

Throughout my forty-plus years of service to the Delaware County community, my unwavering commitment to feeding families has been the driving force behind my actions. Even in moments of frustration, anxiety, or fear of the unknown, I have found that patience and faith are the keys to overcoming obstacles and staying attuned to the whispers of the Holy Spirit.

I recall a pivotal moment in my life when I received misguided advice in the eleventh grade, illustrating the importance of staying true to oneself and not succumbing to peer pressure. Despite the temptation to follow the crowd, I stood firm in my beliefs and chose not to conform, a decision that ultimately shaped my character and strengthened my resolve as a person, wife and a mother..

MOMENTS FOR MOMS II: PEACE, PATIENCE, AND BALANCE

In the busyness of motherhood, faith, and service, I have learned that true strength lies in surrendering to the will of God, embracing patience as a virtue, and trusting in His divine plan for my life and the lives of those around me. May my journey serve as a testament to the power of faith, resilience, and unwavering love in the face of adversity.

MOMENTS FOR MOMS II: PEACE, PATIENCE, AND BALANCE

Lessie Harrison, the ninth child of Milton and Carrie Green from White Oak, Georgia, was raised in a close-knit southern community surrounded by siblings, family, and friends. Growing up with a deep love for God and a passion for serving others, Lessie's path was inspired by the sight of an airplane soaring above the family's fresh produce field, igniting a desire to journey north one day. Following her high school graduation,

MOMENTS FOR MOMS II: PEACE, PATIENCE, AND BALANCE

Lessie, accompanied by her older sister, set off on this quest.

Finding her place in Pennsylvania with her Uncle and Aunt

before embarking on her independent journey, Lessie was

captivated by the work opportunities and lifestyle of the north,

solidifying her roots in a new chapter without ever looking

back.

Lessie encountered her late cherished spouse of four decades,

Bishop James L. Harrison, and together, they nurtured six

children, blessing them with 17 grandchildren and 14 great-

grandchildren who hold their "Nana" in high regard. Lessie and

her husband established and led the True Vine Missionary Full

Gospel Baptist Church, a ministry that extended beyond

traditional boundaries, reaching into the community, across the

state, and even nationwide. Their mission was to demonstrate the love of God and guide other churches in serving the less fortunate in their communities.

As a dedicated food distribution executive with 25 years of service, Lessie shared her passion about serving the community and helping those in need around the southeastern region and nearby areas of Pennsylvania. Throughout her work career, she was diligent in remaining focused on supporting low-income individuals and the most vulnerable areas by ensuring they have access to nutritious food. Her commitment to making a difference in people's lives has driven her to work tirelessly to fight hunger and food insecurity. Today, Lessie still provides essential support to those facing difficult circumstances and believes that everyone deserves access to healthy food and make it happens.

MOMENTS FOR MOMS II: PEACE, PATIENCE, AND BALANCE

CONTACT INFORMATION:

www.grace4purposeco.com

DAY TWELVE- Evangelist Dr. RONJEANNA HARRIS

Breathe~ Reset~ Replenish

"Take Charge of Motherhood"

You're a mother and that is one of your many superpowers. Give yourself a pat on the back. Being a mother is a full-time job. The list of duties is ongoing. You're the sole solution to one or more little humans that depend on you. During this read

MOMENTS FOR MOMS II: PEACE, PATIENCE, AND BALANCE

you will be given some encouraging steps to assist in continuing your journey of motherhood. Getting through the day and week as a mother with a positive mindset and effective productivity is achievable.

Breathe

To all the amazing Queens navigating the journey of motherhood, breathe through life with grace and resilience. Balancing the demands of motherhood with personal aspirations can seem like an insurmountable task, yet it's within these challenges that the opportunity for growth and transformation lies. Embrace each moment with confidence, knowing that every experience shapes you into a more capable, compassionate, and insightful leader—both at home and in your professional endeavors.

MOMENTS FOR MOMS II: PEACE, PATIENCE, AND BALANCE

Strategically integrating self-care into your daily routine isn't just beneficial; it's essential. Carve out time for activities that rejuvenate your spirit and energize your body. This isn't selfishness—it's a strategic move to ensure you're at your best for those who rely on you. Remember, a happy, healthy mother is the cornerstone of a thriving family.

Lastly, never underestimate the power of your support network. Lean on partners, friends, and fellow mothers for advice, encouragement, and a listening ear. Together, you are unstoppable. As you breathe through the ups and downs of motherhood, know that you're not just raising the next generation—you're shaping the future.

MOMENTS FOR MOMS II: PEACE, PATIENCE, AND BALANCE

Reset

We know that motherhood is an adventure filled with its share of ups and downs. It's a journey that continually shapes us, pushing us towards growth and resilience. Yet, amidst the hustle of day-to-day life, we sometimes find ourselves in need of a reset, a moment to pause, breathe, and realign our energies and focus.

Resetting as a mother isn't about finding more time in the day; it's about optimizing the time we have to ensure we're giving the best of ourselves to our families and, importantly, to us. It's about strategic self-care, where even five minutes of mindfulness or a quick walk alone can rejuvenate our spirits and enhance our patience, empathy, and creativity. This strategic approach to resetting allows us to tackle motherhood's

MOMENTS FOR MOMS II: PEACE, PATIENCE, AND BALANCE

challenges with a refreshed perspective, ensuring we're not just surviving but thriving.

Moreover, these reset moments are crucial in setting an example for our children. They learn the importance of self-care, resilience, and the strategic pursuit of happiness and fulfillment from us. By prioritizing these moments, we not only enhance our well-being but also foster an environment where our children can learn the value of balance, self-reflection, and adaptability.

Let's embrace these reset moments with confidence and excitement. By doing so, we're not just bettering ourselves but also paving the way for our children to become resilient, thoughtful, and happy individuals. Here's to being strategic, loving, and absolutely unstoppable resilient in the beautiful journey of motherhood.

MOMENTS FOR MOMS II: PEACE, PATIENCE, AND BALANCE

Replenish

As amazing beings, mothers navigate the delicate balance of nurturing their families and pursuing their own aspirations. It is essential, therefore, to recognize the importance of daily replenishing oneself to maintain this equilibrium. This isn't just about self-care; it's about strategically investing in your well-being to enhance your capacity to inspire, love, and lead.

Firstly, understand that replenishing yourself goes beyond the physical. It includes nurturing your mind and spirit, fostering a sense of peace and resilience. Begin your day with a ritual that centers you—be it meditation, journaling, or a quiet cup of coffee. This sets a positive tone, equipping you to handle the day's challenges with grace and confidence.

MOMENTS FOR MOMS II: PEACE, PATIENCE, AND BALANCE

Incorporate moments of joy and laughter into your day. These are not just fleeting pleasures; they are vital to your emotional and mental health. Whether it's a spontaneous dance party in the living room with your kids or enjoying a chapter of a book in solitude, these moments act as a balm, soothing the day's stresses.

Lastly, embrace the power of community. Lean on fellow mothers, share experiences, and offer support. There's immense strength in knowing you're not navigating this journey alone. Strategic partnerships, in the form of friendships and networks, can be a source of encouragement, advice, and sometimes, much-needed respite.

Remember, replenishing yourself isn't a luxury—it's a necessity. By ensuring you're at your best, you're better equipped to be the incredible mother your family and the world need.

MOMENTS FOR MOMS II: PEACE, PATIENCE, AND BALANCE

1. **Start with a Morning Prayer**: Begin your day with a personal prayer that ignite and structure you. This could be a few minutes of meditation with God almighty. Taking a brisk walk, a cup of your favorite tea, or journaling. The key is to do something that makes you feel centered and ready to tackle the day ahead. Establishing this habit of strong prayer life can help set a positive tone for the entire day.

2. **Nutritious Breakfast**: Never underestimate the power of a healthy breakfast. It fuels your body and brain, helping you to be more alert and patient throughout the day. Incorporating proteins, whole grains, and fruits into your morning meal can keep you energized and prevent mid-morning slumps.

3. **Schedule Me-Time**: It's easy to get caught up in the whirlwind of daily tasks and forget about self-care.

MOMENTS FOR MOMS II: PEACE, PATIENCE, AND BALANCE

Schedule at least 15-30 minutes of "me-time" every day to do something you love – read, take a bath, practice a hobby, or simply sit in silence. This brief respite can significantly boost your mood and energy levels.

4. **Stay Hydrated**: Dehydration can lead to fatigue and irritability. Keep a water bottle handy and sip throughout the day. Infusing your water with fruits or herbs can make this healthy habit more enjoyable and refreshing.

5. **Prioritize Tasks**: Avoid feeling overwhelmed by breaking down your to-do list into manageable tasks. Prioritize them based on urgency and importance. Completing the most critical tasks first can provide a sense of accomplishment and reduce stress.

6. **Take Short Breaks**: Whenever you feel your energy dipping, take a quick break. A short walk, some

stretching, or stepping outside for fresh air can do wonders for your energy levels and productivity.

7. **Connect with Loved Ones**: Spending quality time with family or chatting with a friend can be incredibly rejuvenating. It's a reminder of why you do what you do every day. Even on the busiest days, try to carve out time for these meaningful interactions.

MOMENTS FOR MOMS II: PEACE, PATIENCE, AND BALANCE

Ronjeanna Harris is a God-fearing and chosen ordained Evangelist and affirmed Prophet. Ronjeanna is a devoted wife, mother of six, and grandmother of two. Dr. Ronjeanna is an LPN with over 20 yrs. skill and experience in healthcare. This game-changer is the proud owner of Just Jeanna's Skin Care LLC. Natural Product creator and Formulator was launched as a company in 2018 after much prayer, research, and preparation. After just two years in business, Just Jeanna's Skin Care LLC

got approved to be in the Walmart marketplace in 2020.
Ronjeanna is a 7x Amazon # 1 and international best seller
Author, LPN, and award-winning Certified Wellness Coach
with over 20 years of experience and skill in the healthcare
industry. Just Jeanna's Skin Care LLC offers a host of local,
national, and international services. This trailblazer, in May
2020, started her own nonprofit organization, Jeanna's iFeed,
doing what she loves, which is being a servant. Jeanna's iFeed
has multi award winning nonprofit known for the esteemed
consistency of serving the communities in the Hampton Roads
and Eastern Shore of VA. Kingdom Solutionist coaching and
mentoring services was birthed in 2021. Community serving
and giving back is an honor and passion for Ronjeanna. She has
been serving faithfully is the community since her youth. This
community Philanthropist received her Honorary Doctorate
Degree in Christian Humanities August of 2023. Dr. Ronjeanna

MOMENTS FOR MOMS II: PEACE, PATIENCE, AND BALANCE

is a proud active member of Cornerstone City Refuge Global Alliance (The New City Church of VA) under the Leadership of Apostle Dannie and Pastor Rebecca Ducksworth serving as Evangelist. Dr. Harris prides on effective solutions and healthy collaboration to expands services to our communities. Dr. Harris birthed in 2023 "Ronjeanna Harris Ministries" which purpose and focus is teaching leaders in ministry and believers in the body of Christ the etiquettes along with order of kingdom building and effective outreach under the leading of God. Dr. Harris has received numerous awards, recognitions, news and radio interviews mention for her selfless efforts of impact in community marketplace to build others to their greatest potential. Providing natural wellness solutions is Ronjeanna mission to stand by. Dr. Ronjeanna loves serving firmly believes that God deserves and requires our best and one's lifestyle should represent God in holiness.

CONTACT INFORMATION

Dr. Ronjeanna Harris FB and IG, LinkedIn

www. justjeannas.com

Kingdom Solutionist Coaching & Mentoring on FB

kscoach.mentor@gmail.com

Jeannas iFeed on FB & IG

www.jeannasifeed.org

ronjeanna@jeannasifeed.org

Ronjeanna Harris Ministries on FB and IG

rh.ministries2023@gmail.com

Lefrances Healthcare Education Services LLC on FB

lefranceshealth@gmail.com

DAY THIRTEEN- SHACRE JONES

Get into the Routine of Finding Yourself

Parenting doesn't come with a handbook; at times it can be

challenging. You wear many hats like mom, entrepreneur, wife,

career woman, etc. Some days you'll do a great job and others,

let's just say you're a work in progress. It is during those times

of chaos and being pulled every which way that you need to

find peace, patience, and balance. As a mother I have a blended

family and that in itself can be challenging. A huge challenge

you can face with having a blended family is different

households have a different set of rules. When they come from

the other house it feels like you have to retrain them on what the

rules are in your household. In those moments you must stand

firm by your rules and standards. I had to let my children know

that some things are non-negotiable and not feel bad after

standing my ground. Sometimes it can be hard to discipline our

children because we love them so much, but the Bible tells us in

Revelation 3:19, "Those I love I rebuke and discipline." The

foundation of morals and values starts at home. Apart of co-

parenting is working together for the best interest of the

child(ren) Co-parenting with someone who doesn't understand

the importance of communication between the parents and not

having the children in the middle of adult issues is tough. This can mentally put a lot of stress on you and your child(ren).

Sometimes we think we protect our children by trying to protect them from the issues, however most children know more than we think they know. Keeping the lines of communication with your child is very important. I realized through having open honest conversations with my children that they knew more than I thought they knew, and they understood. There was an old saying, "children are to be seen and not heard," that I grew up on. That saying in my opinion, is so toxic! Your children should have a voice! You don't muzzle a child. I allowed my children to express themselves and their feelings respectfully and we had open dialogue to understand each other's feelings. I had to find that balance because I grew up in a dysfunctional household and I had to unlearn a lot of my learned behaviors. My mother that raised me was very strict and she was a dictator. She had an authoritative parenting style, so parenting was a learning curve for me. A simple strategy I used is I had to learn to be open to listening to my children instead of forcing them to think like I wanted them to think. To be honest I had a conversation with my oldest daughter. I apologized to her for the version of me that she got growing up. I was immature, broken, and had a lot to learn. I did the best I could with what I knew and although I did a great job and she's a great child at 20 years old. My younger children now are getting a better version of me. They are seeing the healed version of me. So you have to find balance and be open to learning new things and unlearning vicious unhealthy cycles in your parenting journey. After being divorced I found myself a single mother until I remarried. There were many challenges that came with going through a divorce. The biggest challenge was the mental and emotional stress that I felt, but even more what my children were experiencing. I had to truly find God and find myself. If it wasn't for prayer and

MOMENTS FOR MOMS II: PEACE, PATIENCE, AND BALANCE

reading the Word of God, I don't know how I would have made it. I was mentally, spiritually, and emotionally drained. I always kept a notebook full of encouraging scriptures on my phone to read when I was having a bad day. My hope was in God. Some of my favorite chapters of scriptures to quote are Psalm 23, Psalm 91, Jeremiah 29:11, and Psalm 46. One that I quoted daily was Psalm 46:5- *God is within her; she will not fail; God will help her at break of day.* Those scriptures got me through a lot of sleepless days and nights. Psalm 46:5 was one of those scriptures that no matter what I was facing as a parent, in my career, or in my marriage reminded me that I am a conqueror, and I am an overcomer because God was with me every step of the way. It merely says "she will not fail" that she was me! That resonated in my spirit day in and day out.

MOMENTS FOR MOMS II: PEACE, PATIENCE, AND BALANCE

I have a saying "speak it until you see it" and I saw it! I saw the hand of God on my life. In addition to finding God, I had to find a good therapist. Growing up in my household we were never taught about therapy, it was frowned upon. Therapy was one of the reasons I'm still standing. Going through therapy and really seeking God for a relationship opened my eyes to so many things. I realized in going through the ugly healing process that throughout my childhood I was functioning in dysfunction. The best thing that ever happened to me in my transition was having the right support. I didn't grow up with family support, so I created my own. I started going to a support group and it was there that I met a group of women that became my sisters. Whenever I needed them, they were always there. They showed up with no questions asked, and I am truly grateful for the relationship that we still share.

MOMENTS FOR MOMS II: PEACE, PATIENCE, AND BALANCE

My support system changed my life, it matters who you're connected to. When you begin to make changes some people, places, and things will now seem so foreign to you. I realized the trauma, dysfunction, brokenness, and healing that my family needed during my process. Embrace the change!! This will give you a great sense of freedom and peace. A great lesson I had to learn as a parent is that you must take time for yourself. I never knew what "self-care" was until later on in my life. I thought being a good mother was having my children all the time and smothering them. But that is so far from the truth! You have to take care of yourself. I used to feel guilty about getting my hair and nails done but every time I walked in the store, I bought something for my children. I had every right to pamper myself every now and then. This helped boost my confidence when I looked and felt pretty.

MOMENTS FOR MOMS II: PEACE, PATIENCE, AND BALANCE

Your mental health is an important part of your self-care because you can't pour from an empty cup. I also found my spark by doing the things I love and trying new things. I encourage you to try something new. My something new was creating a bucket list, and I began to do all of those things on the list that I've always wanted to do. I went to the movies by myself, took myself out to eat, and traveled by myself. This helped me learn to love myself even more. I was exploring me and I was finally able to genuinely enjoy being who I was. As mothers we tend to want to have an "S" on our chest and wear a cape and in that we neglect ourselves, but we must take the time to find balance in our everyday hectic lives. Don't get so wrapped up in parenting that you lose yourself. I'm a true testament to that. When I got divorced, I knew everything I thought I needed to know about my children and being a wife but outside of that who was I?? What am I going to be when I

MOMENTS FOR MOMS II: PEACE, PATIENCE, AND
BALANCE

grow up? I had to find myself in my thirties. Who knew I was

talented, I had a purpose, I was an author, advocate, and that I'd

become the woman I am today? God knew but I had no idea

who I was and what I was supposed to do with my life. I

became the best version of myself when I started to invest in

me. What I did so gracefully for everybody around me I failed

at doing it for myself. There are benefits to loving yourself! We

plan our children's schedule down to the second and if you're

anything like me work is very demanding, so you have to find

balance. Balance for me was creating a routine. Apart from

learning who I was I found that routines work, schedules work,

and organizing things work! This helped me out a lot. When I

found myself slipping away from the things that worked, I knew

depression and stress was overtaking me. This is how I noticed

when I needed to tend to my mental health. Being unorganized

and chaos was a red flag that let me know I was headed in the wrong direction. Be patient with yourself, you are learning and navigating this thing called life like everybody else. One of the biggest lessons I've learned was there's no such thing as perfect or perfection. I struggled most of my life beating myself up because everything had to be "perfect", and I was this perfectionist that had to get everything right! Throw that out the window! When I grasped the fact that it doesn't have to be perfect, but it can be done with decency and with a spirit of excellence, this literally saved my life! I was driving myself to a mental breakdown. If I could leave you with one last thought, taking care of yourself and finding balance, peace, and patience throughout your journey of motherhood and life will allow you to overcome so many challenges and not feel like you're carrying the weight of the world on your shoulders. Bag ladies, release those bags.

MOMENTS FOR MOMS II: PEACE, PATIENCE, AND BALANCE

VISIONARY * MENTOR *COACH * MOTIVATIONAL

SPEAKER * DOMESTIC VIOLENCE ADVOCATE *BEST

SELLING AUTHOR * MIDWIFE *NATIONAL

SPOKESPERSON

MOMENTS FOR MOMS II: PEACE, PATIENCE, AND BALANCE

Shacre Jones is not your average individual. She's a force to be reckoned with - an accomplished author, a captivating motivational speaker, and an unwavering advocate for raising awareness about domestic violence. Residing in the Dover, Delaware region. Shacre Jones is a survivor of domestic abuse and thriving advocate passionate about women evolving after abuse. Through her ministry and writing, she fearlessly uses her voice to encourage, uplift, challenge, and inspire people of all ages. With Jones's remarkable ability to connect with her audience on a deeply emotional level, she transforms into a powerful speaker who brings unparalleled depth and perspective to topics such as faith, family, relationships, domestic violence prevention, and personal development.

Shacre Jones brings 10 years of expertise in the field of domestic violence awareness and prevention. She has been a

MOMENTS FOR MOMS II: PEACE, PATIENCE, AND BALANCE

vocal advocate for survivors of domestic abuse, creating

resources and offering support to those who have experienced

trauma. As the media spokesperson for the All-State Foundation

and National Network to End Domestic Violence (NNEDV)

2015-2017, Jones has made a significant impact. In 2017 her

story of survival was featured in Glamour magazine. Jones

previously served as the Executive Director and domestic

violence advocate with the Empowered Women Ministries,

where she uses her expertise to inspire and empower women to

become the best version of themselves. In 2017 Jones was one

of the leaders that traveled with EWM to Jamaica for a mission

trip to minister to young women in the country.

Additionally, she has traveled the country speaking as an

advocate to help women break the cycle of unhealthy

relationships. Through a holistic approach, she guides topics

such as career advancement, financial literacy, health and

wellness, and self-care. With a passion for helping people reach their highest potential: Jones is an in-demand keynote speaker and workshop facilitator around the country. In 2019 Jones was nominated and won Achi Magazine's Health and Wellness award for sharing her testimony of survival spreading awareness to women all over the world. Jones spearheads the Rebuilding Your Life After Divorce an empowerment group in Delaware, Maryland that helps women who have gone through a divorce empower their lives and start anew. Shacre is an Amazon bestselling author she co-authored The Purposed Woman. Wrote and published My Journey to Healing Journal and A Warriors Prayer Fighting Battles Through Intercessory Prayer. On the horizon are two new Releases Letters To My Younger Self and co- author of Moments For Moms II. Jones remarried in August of 2020 and takes pride in being a loving mother and a wife. Jones and her husband own and operate multiple small businesses in the Delaware region. In her professional career Jones serves in Human Resources management with a passion for recruiting. Shacre Jones has faithfully served in ministry for many years. Since 2016 she serves as a licensed and ordained evangelist. Jones has a marketplace ministry Jones is the founder and visionary for "Life After the Scars". As a midwife to women rebuilding after abusive relationships it is Jones's goal to own and operate transitional housing around the globe.

As Featured in Glamour:
My First Year After Leaving an Abusive Relationship
My First Year After Leaving an Abusive Marriage | Glamour

MOMENTS FOR MOMS II: PEACE, PATIENCE, AND BALANCE

CONTACT INFORMATION:
For more information or to book Shacre Jones for an
engagement, please contact:

Phone: (302) 242-1556
Email: Shacrerjones@gmail.com
Website: WWW.SHACREJONES.COM
Facebook: https://www.facebook.com/ShacrerJones
TikTok: @IamShacrethewarrior

DAY FOURTEEN- Cyteese Alexander

We may bend but we won't break

Hello to all the beautiful moms that are reading this right at this very moment. I want to let you know that it is not by chance you picked up this book. You were meant to be here at this very moment and in this new season that you are in. I want to share with you woman to woman, and mom to mom on what it has been like finding peace, patience, and balance in my hectic life

MOMENTS FOR MOMS II: PEACE, PATIENCE, AND BALANCE

as a mom of 4 children. The work was not easy, but I promise what you get out of finding those things is so rewarding,

The one thing that has been so hard for me was learning how to balance work life and home life. It has not been easy to do. You find yourself trying to please everyone in both parts of your life. One thing that I had to learn and train my mind not to do was overdo myself in the process. When you are burned out you cannot be any good to anyone. I learned to do what I can for the day, and what I can't get done will be there the next day. I have to give myself grace. I cannot overwork myself.

Maintaining and keeping a positive attitude, your heart right, and making sure your mental is okay is just one of many things that can be done to keep that balance within your life. Making sure your mind is clear from all negativities.

MOMENTS FOR MOMS II: PEACE, PATIENCE, AND BALANCE

I want to give you some techniques that have helped me to find my peace and to keep it going on a day-to-day basis. Exercise is just one that I try to do. Walking, going to the gym, etc. I find it easier for me to start having to go early mornings vs afternoon after work. My household is still quiet and if I do it in the mornings I feel I have more energy to kick start my day and before it gets hectic. Prayer has always been my personal anecdotes for my tranquility. I have never gone wrong with using that time after time again. And you will too.

It is very vital to prioritize your mental well-being. Growing up I did not know what mental health was, nor was I taught about how to prioritize it. But as the saying goes, "when you know better, you do better." Now that I do know better, I want all the readers to know just how important it really is.

MOMENTS FOR MOMS II: PEACE, PATIENCE, AND BALANCE

I have overcome so many obstacles in my life. But to overcome them while you have patience is a little different. Having twin boys that was born prematurely and not knowing if one would make it really tested my patience. Thank God for covering them and allowing them to grow up and to beat a lot of those odds that were stacked up against them. It just goes to show and prove that prayer works!! Now, there is a flip side to this. Could we still show patience when they beat those odds just to turn around in their teenage years and have to go through and overcome some of those same issues now. "What did you do Cyteese?," you asked. I speak over them, I pray over them, and I remember what God did back then for them, and I stand on it. And when you speak the Word back to Him it makes having patience just a little bit easier!

MOMENTS FOR MOMS II: PEACE, PATIENCE, AND BALANCE

Your journey may be different than mine, but as moms we still have to find ways to maintain our peace, patience and balance; no matter what our journey looks like.

Here are three tips that I want to leave with you to help maintain your peace, patience and balance. I'm here on this journey with you, don't worry I got you.

1. To maintain your peace everyone is not going to be able to have access to you at any given time. That will burn you out. You must establish boundaries because people will come to dump their stuff on you and you will be left tired. After that you won't have any energy for yourself, your spouse or your children.

MOMENTS FOR MOMS II: PEACE, PATIENCE, AND BALANCE

2. This next one is very important and to be honest, I am not going to say that you will master this every day, but overtime as you develop your relationship with Him you will see why it is important. Learning to take time each day and spending that one-on-one uninterrupted time with the Father and talk to Him you will find it easier to have patience without losing it when inconveniences happen in life.

3. And finally, learning to maintain balance. As moms we have so much that we have to take care of during the day. One thing that will help you with maintain balance is having an agenda or a planner. I used to think I was super woman and that I could have it all in my mind and wouldn't forget anything. Of course, my mind as my planner started to fail me because there was just too much to keep up with. Once I invested in a planner that I noticed my life going a little bit better from day to day.

MOMENTS FOR MOMS II: PEACE, PATIENCE, AND BALANCE

Everyday won't be easy, but with balance and patience, peace is

right there waiting for you!

MOMENTS FOR MOMS II: PEACE, PATIENCE, AND BALANCE

Cyteese Alexander is a wife, and a mother of 4 children. Her journey started different from others; she was a high-school dropout but that did not stop her. She went back and received her GED after giving birth to her first three children. Cyteese is a minister, motivational speaker and a 4x published author; one of which is an Amazon Best-Seller. She has also been nominated 2 years in a row for the ACHI magazine awards. Cyteese is continuing to walk in her purpose and dreams. She has made a commitment to fulfill all that God has put her on this earth to do.

MOMENTS FOR MOMS II: PEACE, PATIENCE, AND BALANCE

CONTACT INFORMATION:

To book a speaking engagement or to connect on other projects.

FB-Cyteese Alexander

IG-Iam_cyteese

Email: iamcyteese@gmail.com

Be on the lookout for the relaunch of her website

iamcyteese.com

DAY FIFTEEN-Juanita N. Woodson

Finding Balance: Navigating Motherhood, Faith, and

Purpose

"Life happens" that's a saying I've heard my mother say

growing up and even now as an adult. There are so many things

that happen in life totally out of our control, we know as mom's

that we have to keep pushing. We learn to find peace in the

midst of chaos. We find patience instead of losing our mind. We

MOMENTS FOR MOMS II: PEACE, PATIENCE, AND BALANCE

find balance when there are a lot of roles to juggle. Finding peace, patience and balance is not always easy, it takes time, healing, and grace. We may not always get it right every single time, but we continue showing up and putting our best foot forward. Not just for us, but for our family, our children and to inspire other moms who may feel like things are just too hard to bear.

I'm a mom to a 16-year-old, and a bonus mom to a 10-year-old. I became a mom right out of graduating high school and there was so much I was uncertain of and had to just learn along the way. Becoming a mom so young made me grow up quick, but I didn't learn the importance of balancing until my son was much older. I found myself working more than one job for years. This meant that I had to spend more time away from him than I

would like. And although I was working a lot I still struggled to
really make ends meet for quite some time.

I had to learn to put needs over wants. Did it benefit us in the
long run to work so many hours day and night, week after week
and not have much to show for it? My journey to learning
balance led me to face myself and hold myself accountable.
There were certain sacrifices that I needed to learn to make so
that it would benefit us in the long run. Learning how to budget
was important. Learning how to say no and understanding that I
needed to prepare for the future and not just right now. I would
find myself wanting to work a second job around the holidays
just to make sure we could have what society makes us feel is a
"great Christmas". As a mother we want to give our children the
world and we can sometimes overwhelm ourselves and lose
balance by comparing our life and what we have to what other

parents may be able to provide. I didn't realize that not only was

it keeping me away from spending additional time with my son,

it also was keeping me from investing time in my purpose, and

walking into who God created me to be which would benefit us

so much more than I could even imagine.

With learning balance, it has a way of bringing peace. In the

midst of life happening, we have to remember that God never

puts more on us than we can bear. Sometimes my peace was

interrupted because I was putting more on my plate than God

even intended for me. 1 Corinthians 14:33 reminds me often

that God is not a God of confusion, but of peace. As a mom, I

learned the importance of taking time to think about a decision

before making it. Not only is this important to maintaining

balance in your household, but it is also helpful in keeping

peace in your mind, and even in your home.

MOMENTS FOR MOMS II: PEACE, PATIENCE, AND BALANCE

The challenge was doing this as a single mom with one income. It was hard to say no to those job opportunities that would bring additional income in. I started to use that extra time that I now had and get more consistent with going to church and separating myself from things and people that weren't benefiting my growth as a woman and as a mother. It took patience, not just with myself but also in trusting the plan that God had for my life. But the more I started to trust God, the more things became clearer to me. I eventually went on to write my first book, "Don't Go That Way: Protect Your Purpose" which changed the trajectory of my life.

As I started to grow in my purpose, I didn't realize how easy it would be for me to fall back into that same pitfall of having no balance if I didn't establish boundaries. Between working a full-time job and trying to balance the world of being an entrepreneur, I started to see that balance I had start to slip

away. I had a lot of pieces moving in life, but I had to make sure

I stay connected to the source of my strength, the Lord.

It is vitally important for mothers to find time for self-care. That

self-care does not always mean getting a manicure or a pedicure

or finding your way to Sunday Brunch. Self-care can also mean

surrounding yourself with the right people, people that can pour

into you. People that can pray for you. It can also mean

cleansing your social media timelines. I learned that the most

important self-care for me was staying grounded in my

relationship with God.

I often remind myself of my favorite scripture, Jeremiah 29:11,

"For I know the plans I have for you, plans to prosper and not to

harm you. Plans to give you hope for a future." There were

MOMENTS FOR MOMS II: PEACE, PATIENCE, AND BALANCE

times when I had to find my way back to feeling like I had hope for a future after having my son. Those times where I felt like I was losing my mind, peace and balance, this scripture always brings me back to that place of remembering that God has good plans for my life. It took me a long time to understand that even in all that I went through, God will still turn things around for my good and my son's life too. I struggled, and I didn't always get it right, but I didn't give up.

Mama's find that scripture, that quote, that support group that will help remind you when you feel like you are losing your balance that God has plans to prosper you. Remind yourself often that God makes all things work together for your good, not some things, but all things. Also remember not to put more on your plate than God ever intended for you to bear. Be mindful of the spaces, places, and things that you accept in your life because it doesn't just affect you. God does not cause confusion, so seek Him first for all things!

Romans 8:28

"And we know that for those who love God all things work together for good, for those who are called according to his purpose."

MOMENTS FOR MOMS II: PEACE, PATIENCE, AND BALANCE

Juanita N. Woodson, a devoted wife and nurturing mother, stands as a beacon of inspiration in both her personal and professional life. As a best-selling author, she has skillfully woven her words into tales that captivate the hearts and minds of readers around the world.

MOMENTS FOR MOMS II: PEACE, PATIENCE, AND BALANCE

In addition to her literary accomplishments, Juanita is the visionary owner of Grace 4 Purpose Publishing Co. LLC. With a passion for empowering others, she dedicates her time to coaching aspiring authors, guiding them on their journey to not only write but also successfully publish their own stories. Her commitment to nurturing the creative spirit within each individual is reflected in the diverse and impactful works that emerge under her guidance.

Beyond the realm of publishing, Juanita is a multifaceted entrepreneur who seamlessly balances the roles of mentor, leader, and advocate. Her dedication to the written word is matched only by her commitment to fostering a community where aspiring writers can flourish and find their voices.

In her journey to leave an indelible mark on the literary landscape, Juanita N. Woodson continues to inspire, uplift, and

MOMENTS FOR MOMS II: PEACE, PATIENCE, AND BALANCE

empower those around her, leaving an enduring legacy of

creativity, resilience, and purpose.

Connect with Juanita N. Woodson:

IG: @_juanitanicole_

IG: @grace4purposeco

Facebook: Juanita Nicole Woodson

TikTok: @authorjuanitanicole

Email: Contacts@grace4purposeco.com

Website: www.grace4purposeco.com

MOMENTS FOR MOMS II: PEACE, PATIENCE, AND BALANCE

Grace4Purposeco.com